MATT AND T

ULTI
FOOTBALL HER

RASHFORD
DELE ALLI

FROM THE PLAYGROUND
TO THE PITCH

DINO

A DINO BOOK

First published in the UK in 2020 by Dino Books,
an imprint of Bonnier Books UK,
The Plaza, 535 King's Road, London SW10 0SZ
Owned by Bonnier Books,
Sveavägen 56, Stockholm, Sweden

@dinobooks
@footieheroesbks
heroesfootball.com
www.bonnierbooks.co.uk

Text © Matt Oldfield 2020

ISBN: 9781789463866

Design by www.envydesign.co.uk

Rashford first published in 2020
Paperback ISBN: 9781789462340
Ebook ISBN: 9781789462357

Dele Alli first published in 2020
Paperback ISBN: 9781789462425
Ebook ISBN: 9781789462432

British Library Cataloguing-in-Publication Data:
A catalogue record for this book is available from the British Library.

Printed and bound in Great Britain by Clays Ltd, Elcograf S.p.A.

1 3 5 7 9 10 8 6 4 2

MIX
Paper from
responsible sources
FSC® C018072

ULTIMATE
FOOTBALL HEROES

Matt Oldfield delivers sports writing workshops in schools, and is the author of *Unbelievable Football* and *Johnny Ball: Accidental Football Genius*. Tom Oldfield is a freelance sports writer and the author of biographies on Cristiano Ronaldo, Arsène Wenger and Rafael Nadal.

Cover illustration by Dan Leydon
To learn more about Dan visit danleydon.com
To purchase his artwork visit etsy.com/shop/footynews

RASHFORD

TABLE OF CONTENTS

CHAPTER 1 – **UNITED'S PENALTY KING IN PARIS** 9

CHAPTER 2 – **FRONT-GARDEN FOOTBALL** 16

CHAPTER 3 – **FLETCHER MOSS RANGERS** 22

CHAPTER 4 – **A HAT-TRICK FROM A NEW HERO** 29

CHAPTER 5 – **BUSY BOY** 35

CHAPTER 6 – **MADE FOR MANCHESTER UNITED** 41

CHAPTER 7 – **ROONEY AND THE NEW RONALDO** 46

CHAPTER 8 – **GROWING UP FAST** 52

CHAPTER 9 – **SIZE, STRENGTH AND SPEED** 59

CHAPTER 10 – **FROM NUMBER 10 TO NUMBER 9** 65

CHAPTER 11 – **DREAM DEBUT 1** 71

CHAPTER 12 – **DREAM DEBUT 2** 78

CHAPTER 13 – **MANCHESTER DERBY MAGIC** 84

CHAPTER 14 – **TROPHY TIME** 92

CHAPTER 15 – **EURO 2016** 99

CHAPTER 16 – **LEARNING (FROM A LEGEND)** 106

CHAPTER 17 – **EUROPEAN GLORY** 113

CHAPTER 18 – **NEW SEASON, SAME POSITION** 120

CHAPTER 19 – **2018 WORLD CUP** 127

CHAPTER 20 – **UNITED'S NEW NUMBER 10** 136

CHAPTER 21 – **SCORING AGAIN UNDER SOLSKJÆR** 141

CHAPTER 22 – **FINDING THE NET IN THE NATIONS LEAGUE** 148

CHAPTER 23 – **UNITED'S STAR STRIKER** 155

CHAPTER 1

UNITED'S PENALTY KING IN PARIS

6 March 2019, Parc des Princes, Paris

'A dreadful night for Manchester United' – that's what the newspapers said after PSG's simple first leg win at Old Trafford. 'They'll need a miraculous comeback now to keep their Champions League campaign alive.'

Not only were United 2–0 down as they travelled to Paris, but they were also missing three of their most important attackers. Anthony Martial and Jesse Lingard had both picked up injuries, while Paul Pogba had been given a red card.

What a disaster! That only left the manager, Ole

Gunnar Solskjær, with two fit and available forwards: Romelu Lukaku and United's local boy wonder, Marcus Rashford.

If anyone could save the day with a moment or two of magic, it was Marcus. He had done it many times before for United in the Europa League, starting at the age of only eighteen, so why couldn't he now do the same in the Champions League?

Marcus was ready to step up and shine. Under United's new manager, he had found his scoring form again, with seven goals already. In the Premier League, the FA Cup – now the Champions League would be next.

'Let's do this!' he told Romelu as they took up their positions on the pitch.

Although Marcus sounded as confident as ever, he knew that it wouldn't be easy. Even without Neymar Jr, the PSG team was still packed full of world-class talent: Gianluigi Buffon, Thiago Silva, Dani Alves, Marco Verratti, ex-United man Ángel Di María and, of course, Kylian Mbappé.

Back in 2017, Mbappé had beaten Marcus to win

the Golden Boy award for the best young player in Europe. Since then, he had also won two French league titles and the World Cup with France, as well as scoring his team's second goal at Old Trafford. Now, it was time for Marcus – and United – to bounce back.

As soon as the match kicked off, Marcus was racing around causing problems for the PSG defence. When Thilo Kehrer saw United's speedy Number 10 sprinting towards him, he panicked. His pass fell between Buffon and Thiago Silva, perfect for Romelu to intercept. *GOAL – 1–0!*

'Come on!' United's star strikeforce celebrated together.

Minutes later, Marcus used his pace and power to beat Kehrer to the ball and then tried to cross it to Romelu.

'Unlucky!' Solskjær clapped and cheered on the sidelines. 'Keep going!'

Again and again, Marcus was making Kehrer look like a fool, but unless it led to a goal, it wouldn't really matter. And when PSG equalised, that meant

United now needed to score three to win...

Marcus wasn't giving up, though. As he dribbled into the penalty area, he could hear Romelu calling for it in the middle. Cross or shoot? Cross or shoot? In the end, he couldn't make up his mind and got it all wrong. His mixture of cross and shoot curled well wide of the far post.

'Hey, I was here!' Romelu cried out near the penalty spot. He wasn't happy with his strike partner.

So the next time Marcus got the ball, he made up his mind straight away. Even though he was a long way from goal, he was going to shoot. BANG! He put so much whip and dip and swerve on the ball that it squirmed out of Buffon's gloves. And Romelu reacted first to pounce on the rebound. *GOAL – 2–1!*

'Nice one, Rash!' he high-fived Marcus as they ran back for the restart.

One more – that was all United needed now to pull off a miraculous Champions League comeback. Twice Marcus thought that he was through on goal, but both times the linesman's flag went up at the last second. *Offside!*

'Arghh!' he kicked the air in frustration. Time was running out.

And with ten minutes to go, it looked like Mbappé was about to end United's hopes. As he controlled the ball on the edge of the box, he only had David de Gea to beat, but somehow, he stumbled and fell.

Phew! Marcus breathed a big sigh of relief and then refocused his mind. The comeback was still on for United, if only they could create one last chance...

As Diogo Dalot ran forward from right-back, Marcus and Romelu were both in the box, hoping for a dangerous cross. Instead, the Portuguese defender went for goal. His shot deflected off a PSG player and flew high and wide. 'At least we've got a corner,' Marcus thought to himself, but Diogo thought differently.

'Penalty!' he screamed, pointing at his arm. 'Handball!'

Really? After a long and agonising wait while the referee checked VAR, at last it was given – a last-minute penalty for United!

Wow, it was a harsh call, but Marcus wasn't

complaining. Now it was his responsibility to step up and score to send United into the Champions League quarter-finals. As the PSG players protested, he tried his best to stay calm and focused. Put the ball in the net – that was all he had to do.

Marcus had been in high pressure positions like this before, most recently at the 2018 World Cup with England. He had scored in the shoot-out against Colombia; and now he had to do it again.

When the referee blew his whistle, Marcus started his well-practised penalty routine:

Four little shuffles to the left,
then short steps forward to try to fool the keeper,
and then *BANG!*

Buffon did dive the right way, but he had no chance of stopping it. Marcus had struck his penalty with way too much power; it was simply unstoppable.

Goooooooooooooooooooooaaaaaaaaaaaaaaaaalllllllllllllllllllllllllll!!!!!!!!!!!!!!!!!!!!!!

'What a penalty!' Diogo shouted as he chased

Marcus over to the fans by the corner flag. Their comeback was complete.

And what a night. Marcus Rashford: Manchester United Champions League Hero was just the latest step in his amazing football journey. A journey that had started eighteen years earlier in his family's front garden.

CHAPTER 2

FRONT-GARDEN FOOTBALL

From the very first time he saw it on TV, Marcus was mesmerised by football. As a baby in his mother's arms, he stared at the figures on the screen, wearing their red shirts and white shorts, running around a big green space, and kicking a small white round object. What was this weird and wonderful thing?

'Look Mum, he loves Manchester United already!' Marcus' big brother Dwaine cried out cheerfully.

Melanie smiled and held her youngest son up high like a trophy. 'That's my boy!' she said, looking lovingly at his happy little face.

The Rashfords lived in Wythenshawe, which was proud Manchester United territory, especially in the late 1990s. While their local rivals, Manchester City, were battling down in the second division, United were lifting the Premier League title for the fifth time, plus the FA Cup and the UEFA Champions League.

'I can't believe we won The Treble,' Dwaine marvelled, almost as if he had been one of the players out there on the pitch. 'What a club. What a season!'

United were the greatest team in England, and also the greatest team in the whole wide world. Well, according to Dwaine and Dane, anyway, and Marcus always believed his brothers.

They were his heroes, and as soon as he could walk, Marcus followed them around as much as he could. But there was one place where his mum wouldn't let him go – outside.

'See ya later, lil' man!' His brothers waved, closing the front door behind them.

Where were they going, and why couldn't he go with them? Marcus had spotted the football in Dwaine's hands. It looked like it came from that weird and wonderful game they had watched together on TV.

'Hey, wait for me – I want to play too!' Marcus decided, and he waddled over to the front door to follow them. But as hard as he tried, it wouldn't open.

'Woah, where do you think you're going?' Melanie appeared, scooping him up into her arms. 'Are you trying to escape again, Mister? Look, we can watch your brothers from the window…'

Dwaine and Dane hadn't gone far; they were just having a kickaround with their friends in the small front garden. While they showed off all their tricks and flicks, Marcus stared and stared, as if the living room window was another TV screen.

Front-garden football looked like so much fun! He couldn't wait for the day when he would be allowed to join in. But when would that be?

'Please!' he begged his brothers after his third birthday. They had been teaching him to kick and control the ball in the kitchen while their mum was out, but now he was ready to show off his skills *outside*.

But Dwaine and Dane both shook their heads.

'Sorry Marcus, not yet – you're still too young to play with us big boys. Maybe next time, yeah?'

However, when the next time arrived, their answer was still no. And the next time, and the next time… It was so unfair – he was nearly four years old now! So why couldn't he just join in for a little bit of front-garden football? Marcus was willing to do anything, even go in goal if he had to.

'Fine, you can play,' Dwaine gave in eventually, 'but no crying to Mum if you get hurt, okay?'

'Okay!'

And so, at last, Marcus's front garden football career began.

At first, it was all a bit overwhelming for him. His brothers and their friends towered over him and charged around him like wild horses on that small square of grass. It was as if Marcus wasn't even there. Or as if he were an obstacle that was in the way.

'Watch out!' the big boys warned, nearly knocking him to the floor.

Marcus moved out of their path, but he didn't

walk away. This was front-garden football; he just needed a moment to get used to it.

'Over here – pass!' he desperately wanted to shout, but he was too shy to say it out loud. Plus, Marcus knew that if he did anything annoying, his brothers would send him back inside straight away. He really didn't want that.

'But at this rate, they're never going to give me a turn!' Marcus moaned to himself. He didn't give up, though. He soon swapped his gloomy frown for a fired-up glare. 'If I want that ball, then I'm going to have to win it for myself!'

Marcus would just have to be brave amongst the big boys. With a bold dart, he snatched the ball from under Dwaine's foot.

'Hey!' he complained. 'What are you playing at, bro?'

'It's my turn,' Marcus replied determinedly.

Right, now what? He had the ball, but if he didn't do something quickly, one of the big boys would steal it back. Marcus tried to remember some of the skills that he had watched them do through the window. This was his chance to show that he could do them too.

Flick! with his right foot,

Flick! with his left foot,

Flick! with his right knee,

Flick! with his left knee,

Flick pass! with his right heel, back to his brother.

'Not bad,' even Dwaine had to admit.

After that, the big boys changed their minds about Marcus. It turned out that he wasn't just an annoying little boy who was getting in the way; he was a talented young footballer, just like the rest of them.

'Here you go, Marcus – let's see what you've got!'

Soon, he was allowed to go with his brothers to the local Mersey Bank Playing Fields, although 'only to watch'. But while Dwaine and Dane were playing big eleven-a-side matches with their mates, Marcus practised his ball skills on his own on the sidelines, preparing for the day when he would be old enough to join a football team too.

CHAPTER 3

FLETCHER MOSS RANGERS

The Rashford family didn't have a lot of money, but they managed to find enough for young Marcus to go to football training. After all, it was his favourite thing in the whole wide world, and he was clearly very talented too.

'Good luck, son!' Melanie said, giving her youngest son a kiss. She had to go to work, so Dwaine would be taking Marcus along instead.

'Thanks, Mum!' he replied, buzzing with excitement.

Now that he was five, Marcus was old enough to join a local football club called Fletcher Moss Rangers. But first, he had to prove that he was good enough to play for one of Manchester's top youth teams. Wes Brown, the United defender, had started at Fletcher Moss, and now the club had a strong reputation for developing top young players.

'Top young players like me!' Marcus thought to himself on the way to the Mersey Bank Playing Fields.

He couldn't wait to get started. As his boots sank into the bobbly grass, it felt like he was taking the first step on a grand football journey. First, Fletcher Moss Rangers, then Manchester United and England, just like Wes Brown.

'Welcome, Marcus,' the coach, Mark Gaynord said, shaking his hand. 'I hope you're ready to have some fun today!'

Marcus nodded shyly, as a smile spread across his face.

'Great, then let's get started!'

Dwaine had played enough front-garden football with his brother to know that he was a promising young player, but he was curious to see how Marcus would compare against other kids his own age. It didn't take Dwaine long to see that his brother stood out high above the rest.

And the Fletcher Moss coaches saw it too. From the moment that Marcus first touched the ball, Gaynord could see that he had a natural gift for the game. It was as if he came alive with a football at his feet, his whole body suddenly working in smooth, skilful motion.

The head up, turning, looking out for defenders to beat and teammates to pass to.

The arms out, offering balance through all the twists and turns of the dribble.

The legs pumping, driving him goalwards at top speed.

The feet dancing, moving the ball with such grace and ease until at last, BANG!

Goooooooooooooooooooooaaaaaaaaaaaaaaaaaalllllllllllll llllllllllllll!!!!!!!!!!!!!!!!!!!!

Gaynord had coached many talented kids before, but no-one quite like Marcus. 'That boy is a superstar in the making,' the Fletcher Moss coach told himself, and he didn't doubt that for a second. The kid's ability was astonishing. Marcus had already mastered so many tricks and flicks at the age of five!

'How did he learn to dribble like that?' Gaynord asked Dwaine in awe.

'He probably saw me doing it in the park!' his brother said with a cheeky smile and then shrugged. 'Or maybe it was on FIFA, actually...'

Marcus just seemed to soak up football skills like a sponge, whether he was watching his heroes on TV, playing video games, or playing for Fletcher Moss Rangers in real life.

'That's it, yes – brilliant!'

As Marcus's coach, Gaynord soon gave up on teaching him the basics; he was already too good for that. Instead, he focused on finding ways to stop his young superstar in the making from getting bored because even in their twenty-minute matches, Marcus was scoring goal after goal after goal. Often, it looked more like a one-boy skill show than an actual football match.

'Okay, that's enough,' Gaynord would call out when the scoreline was starting to get embarrassing. 'Give some of the others a chance!'

At that stage, Marcus would drop deeper and

switch to setting up his teammates with assist after assist after assist. The Fletcher Moss coach felt sorry for the other teams they faced; they simply didn't stand a chance.

So, how could Gaynord help Marcus to become even better? By setting him new skills challenges to complete, the coach decided.

'So, have you been practising that Maradona spin I showed you?' he asked before kick-off.

Marcus had been working on it all week at the Mersey Bank Playing Fields and then back home in the front garden too. But he didn't all say that to his coach; instead, he just nodded calmly and confidently. Gaynord would just have to wait and see...

As soon as he got the ball, Marcus burst forward on the attack. He was over the halfway line and hurtling towards the penalty area when, at last, a defender came across to close him down...

Right, this was it! Usually, Marcus would dribble around his opponents, or just kick it past the defender and use his speed to reach it first. But not this time; no, he had a new trick to try out. Just when it looked like he was going to crash straight into the defender, Marcus dragged the ball back with his right foot, spun his whole body around, and dragged the ball forward with his left foot. *Olé!*

'Maradona Spin!' Gaynord thought to himself, clapping even louder than usual.

Marcus was away, past the first tackle, but there was another one on the way. No problem! He had something extra up his sleeve to add to his coach's challenge. As the second defender slid in, Marcus dragged the ball back behind him and went the other way.

'Cruyff Turn!' Gaynord gasped. It was extraordinary. How had he learnt that trick too?!

The coach looked across at Marcus's mum, who had managed to get the day off work to watch her son play. 'I've never seen a kid that young play like this before,' he admitted with an amazed look still on his face.

Melanie just laughed. 'Oh come on, Mark – you must see little superstars all the time!'

But the Fletcher Moss coach wasn't joking around,

or being dramatic; he was deadly serious. He had been involved in football all his life, so he knew what he was talking about when he said, 'No, honestly, your lad is going to play for Manchester United and England one day.'

CHAPTER 4

A HAT-TRICK FROM A NEW HERO

Marcus had to touch the red plastic seat behind
him, just to make sure that it wasn't a dream.
Yes, he really was at Old Trafford, about to watch
Manchester United play!

'So, what do you think?' Dwaine asked as he lifted
his brother up onto the seat so that he could see the
huge green space below.

But Marcus didn't reply; he was too busy staring
down at the players on the pitch, and spotting all of
his heroes:

There was Ryan Giggs – Number 11,

Fletcher Moss's own Wes Brown – Number 24,

Ole Gunnar Solskjær – Number 20,

And their star striker, Ruud van Nistelrooy –
Number 10!

Hopefully, one day, he would be down there
himself, warming up for United.

Even if Marcus had heard Dwaine's question, he
wouldn't have been able to answer it. With so much
to see and soak up, he was lost for words!

And even if he had replied, his big brother probably
wouldn't have heard him anyway. The atmosphere in
the stadium was electric, with the 60,000 United fans
forming a noisy wall of red. Everyone was looking
forward to an exciting European night. Manchester
United were taking on Spanish giants Real Madrid in
the Champions League quarter-finals.

After losing the away leg 3–1, United had lots of
work to do at Old Trafford. But the belief was still
there, buzzing in the Manchester air.

Come On You Reds!

UNI-TED! UNI-TED!

As Marcus looked around and listened, he couldn't
stop smiling. Watching his favourite team live was
even better than he had imagined!

Although it was a great night for Marcus, it turned out to be a bad one for Manchester United. Their defence was destroyed by the best striker in the whole wide world – Ronaldo. Well, that was what Dwaine said, anyway, and after that night, Marcus agreed with his brother.

First, the Brazilian raced away from Rio Ferdinand and fired a swerving, dipping shot past Fabien Barthez. *1–0 to Real Madrid!*

Then he burst between the United centre-backs to get on the end of Roberto Carlos's cross. *2–1 to Real Madrid!*

And finally, he unleashed a long-range shot that rocketed into the top corner. *3–2 to Real Madrid!*

David Beckham came on for United and scored two goals to make it 4–3, but really it was Ronaldo's night. He was the hat-trick hero, and the best player on the pitch. Even the United fans had clapped when he scored that third thunderstrike.

'Fair play,' Marcus heard the supporters around him say. 'He's a class act, that Ronaldo!'

Marcus and Dwaine were both disappointed

that their team had crashed out of the Champions League, but they returned home with lots of stories and memories, and a new hero to admire.

'Bro, come and check this out!' Dwaine called out from the family computer.

Together, they spent many happy hours watching highlights of Ronaldo on YouTube. It didn't matter if he was starring for Barcelona, Inter Milan, Real Madrid, or Brazil. They were hooked. There were so many videos, so many goals, and – best of all, in Marcus's opinion – so many skills!

The silky taps of the ball,

the sudden bursts of speed,

the body swerves,

and, of course, the stepovers!

To the right, to the left, to the right again, then BANG! – GOAL!

Marcus was more mesmerised than ever. What a player! Out on the pitch, Ronaldo always looked so free – free to try new tricks, free to express himself and free to entertain. He made football look like so much fun.

'Let's watch the Lazio video again!' Marcus suggested almost every single night.

That was one of his favourite clips, from the 1998 UEFA Cup Final, when Ronaldo was playing up front for Inter Milan. They won 3–0 and the Brazilian scored a great goal, where he dribbled around the keeper. But that wasn't the part that Marcus really wanted to watch. No, he was much more interested in seeing the skills show.

'This is it… this bit now!' He pointed at the screen, his excitement growing.

Despite having a Lazio defender tackling him from either side, Ronaldo somehow kept hold of the ball, thanks to some really fast and fancy footwork.

Tap, tap, drag-back, turn, then an Elástico to escape…

And with another calm flick of the foot, he passed the ball onto his teammate.

'Unbelievable!' Marcus marvelled. No matter how many times he watched the clip, it just got better and better. Even when they tried to foul him, the Lazio defenders still couldn't stop him.

But how did Ronaldo do it? There was only one way to find out – time to practise! Marcus grabbed his ball and rushed out into the front garden. From now on, he was going to play the game just like his new hero, however long it took him to learn all the skills.

Marcus dribbled down the left wing and into the penalty area...

Stepover to the left, stepover to the right,

Stepover to the left, shift to the right...

BANG! – GOAL!

Marcus was through, one on one with the keeper...

Body swerve to the left,

Body swerve to the right...

Then, with the keeper lying fooled on the floor, he simply had to tap the ball into the empty net. *GOAL!*

'Wow, so where did you learn those new dance moves then?' his Fletcher Moss coach asked when he first showed them off at training.

'From Ronaldo,' Marcus replied proudly. 'He's my new favourite player now!'

CHAPTER 5

BUSY BOY

Word soon spread about the Little Ronaldo starring up front for Fletcher Moss Under-7s. It wasn't just his bright yellow shirt that was catching everyone's eye. When the team won a big tournament in Manchester, there was a whole crowd of scouts there to watch Marcus. They came from top clubs all over the north of England:

Newcastle,

Crewe,

Everton,

Liverpool,

Manchester City...

And, best of all, Manchester United!

So, was Marcus going to become the latest Fletcher Moss player to move to Old Trafford? The club's scout was certainly very impressed. The boy wonder ticked all the right boxes:

✓ Skill

✓ Speed

✓ Good attitude

✓ Good awareness

✓ Great movement

That last one was really important, but luckily, Marcus was a natural mover, who had also spent hours watching and then copying his hero, Ronaldo. So, with or without the ball, he glided across the grass gracefully, with pace and power. Full marks!

Marcus was delighted when his favourite team invited him to come and train at their Moss Side development centre. 'Yes please!' he replied eagerly.

Suddenly, Marcus was a very busy boy, with a full football schedule:

Training at Liverpool,

Training at Manchester United,

Playing matches for Fletcher Moss Rangers,

Kicking a ball around in the playground at Button Lane Primary School,

Kicking a ball around with his mates at Mersey Bank Playing Fields,

Oh – and a little bit of eating and sleeping in between!

'You must be exhausted after playing all that football,' Gaynord suggested to Marcus at the start of the Fletcher Moss training session.

But it didn't look that way as their young star got the ball and dribbled towards goal at top speed, his body swerving and his feet dancing. It was like there was no end to his energy!

It looked like there was no end to his ability either. The coach could already see that Marcus's time at Liverpool and United was turning him into an even better player. Back at Fletcher Moss, everything was far too easy for him. The other players might as well have been cones for him to dribble through; they had no chance of stopping him. Gaynord knew that it wouldn't be long before the boy left for good.

But where would Marcus go? Such a talented youngster had so many options. With both big Manchester clubs chasing him, he decided to try training at City too.

That might sound like a strange decision for a mad United fan to make, but the Rashford family had just moved to a new house. Their new home was now five miles away from United's training ground, The Cliff, and his mum couldn't drive. City's Platt Lane Complex, on the other hand, was just around the corner.

Platt Lane was so much easier for Marcus to get to, and it helped that Manchester City were desperate to sign him. The club had climbed back up to the Premier League and their manager, Kevin Keegan, was really giving their young players a chance. Shaun Wright-Phillips, Joey Barton, Nedum Onuoha, Stephen Jordan – they had all come through the club's academy and now they were starring for the first team.

'That could be you one day!' the City youth coaches told Marcus.

Although that was an exciting idea, Marcus was still secretly hoping to play for Manchester United one day.

He couldn't sign with any club until his ninth birthday, but as that day grew closer, United upped their efforts. They weren't going to let their local rivals, City, swoop in and steal such a top young talent. No way! There had to be something that they could do to keep Marcus at their club. If he was finding it hard to get to The Cliff, then they would just have to find another way to get him there…

'Of course, no problem,' Dave Horrocks, the Fletcher Moss chairman, said straight away when United asked if he could bring Marcus and his mum along to the club's main training ground.

Horrocks was always happy to help his young players, plus it was an amazing opportunity to visit The Cliff, the place where the famous 'Class of 92' had started their incredible football careers – David Beckham, Ryan Giggs, Paul Scholes, Nicky Butt, and Gary and Phil Neville.

'Are you excited, lad?' Horrocks asked in the car on the way to The Cliff. 'Because I am!'

On the back seat, Marcus nodded and smiled with his usual calm confidence. Yes, it was going to be a test, but a football test, not a maths test! There was nothing for him to worry about. He was excited, and he was ready to make his Manchester United dream come true.

CHAPTER 6

MADE FOR MANCHESTER UNITED

As he walked out onto the training ground pitches, Marcus felt a buzz flow through his body like a bolt of electricity. Mr Horrocks was right; there was definitely something special about this place. This was it – his big moment, training at the home of the mighty Manchester United. He was following in the footsteps of legends like Becks, Giggsy and Scholesy. Unbelievable!

Marcus wasn't letting himself get carried away, though. He knew that he still had a very long way to go if he wanted to one day become a United hero. This was just the start, the first step up from Fletcher Moss.

But it was going to be a very big step all the
same – ginormous, in fact. At The Cliff, Marcus
would be competing against lots of other amazing
young attackers – the best in the city, maybe
even the whole country. What if the club's youth
coaches didn't think he was good enough? What
if they decided not to give him a chance? All
he could do was work hard and play his most
impressive football.

'You've got this, bro,' Dwaine and Dane had told
him before he had left home that morning. They
believed in him, which made Marcus believe in
himself too.

'Welcome to Manchester United!' the coaches
said, shaking his hand and smiling warmly. 'Right,
let's get you playing some football...'

Judging by that first training session, Marcus
wasn't going anywhere – he was made to play for
Manchester United! Their top youth coach, René
Meulensteen, really believed in developing each
player's individual skills for as long as possible, from
the Under-7s all the way up to the first team.

'That's it – one touch to control. Now dribble forward through the cones, moving the ball from foot to foot, keeping it close to your boot… Brilliant, Marcus – well done! Come on lads, the new boy's showing you how it's done!'

It was the perfect environment for Marcus to learn and improve. Because instead of being told to pass the ball every time he touched it, he was encouraged to take his time, be creative and think for himself. What was the best way to get that ball in the net and win the game? He was free to try new tricks, free to express himself and free to entertain, just like his hero, Ronaldo.

'You looked like you were having fun out there today,' Horrocks said on the drive back home.

This time, Marcus didn't just nod and smile. 'Yeah, it was sooooo good!' he replied, the words bursting out of his mouth with joy. 'At first, I thought it was going to be a bit boring, but Coach got us doing all these really fun skills drills, and then we played a match, 5 vs 5, and I scored six goals, and then…'

Melanie was delighted to see her son looking and
sounding so happy. After a few weeks of training
with both Manchester clubs, Marcus knew, without
any doubt, which training programme he preferred.

'I'll become a better footballer at United,' he told
Horrocks. 'That's where I want to be.'

His family agreed, and not just because they were
United fans. They worried that some other clubs
might try to take away Marcus's unique playing style
– the body swerves, the bursts of speed, the skills,
the stepovers. But United wouldn't. At The Cliff, the
coaches would get the best out of his amazing ability
and turn him into a top, top player. Yes, Marcus was
made for Manchester United.

'Right, United it is then!' Whenever he could,
Horrocks drove Marcus to his training sessions at
The Cliff. But when he couldn't, the boy had to
make the adventure across Manchester with one of
his brothers, or even on his own when he was old
enough. Struggling with the weight of his heavy kit
bag, he took one bus into the city centre and then
another out to Salford. After a tough training session

and a long bus ride back home, he would crawl into bed, happy but exhausted.

Luckily, that didn't last for too long. By the time Marcus officially joined Manchester United, aged nine, Dwaine had passed his driving test and bought a car to take him to training. Phew!

'Cheers, bro!'

'No problem. You can pay me back for all the petrol when you're earning £50,000 a week!' Dwaine joked.

Now, Marcus was all set to become a superstar in red, bringing goals and glory to Old Trafford. On the very day that he signed for Manchester United, it just so happened that the first team were training there at The Cliff. What were the chances? It was meant to be!

Van Nistelrooy, Solskjær, Scholesy and Giggsy – they were all right there, just a few pitches away, showing Marcus exactly what he was aiming towards.

CHAPTER 7

ROONEY AND THE NEW RONALDO

By the time that Marcus turned ten, however, he had two more Manchester United heroes: Wayne Rooney and the new Ronaldo.

Cristiano was Portuguese rather than Brazilian, and he was a winger rather than a striker, but just like the old(er) Brazilian Ronaldo, he loved to entertain and show off his silky skills. In fact, out on the pitch, Cristiano probably did even more stepovers.

'Woah, look at his legs go!' Marcus marvelled as he watched YouTube videos with his brothers. As he attacked with the ball, Cristiano's feet were a blur of movement, dancing from side to side. It was all too much for the dizzy defenders. GOAL!

Marcus did his best to copy 'Wazza' and Cristiano. As he was a United fan, they would have been his heroes anyway, but it certainly helped that he got to see them up close at The Cliff, working hard and getting better and better. Sometimes, Marcus would sneak into the gym and sit and watch Cristiano practising a certain skill on repeat until he had perfected it – jumping up for headers, taking free kicks. Didn't he get bored of doing the same thing again and again and again? No, because he was so determined to be the best.

That inspired young Marcus to keep practising his own skills as often as possible, whether he was:

Training at the United academy,

Challenging himself against Dwaine and the other big boys,

Playing all day long with mates his own age at the Mersey Bank Playing Fields,

Or even doing keepy-uppies with a tennis ball on the way to school.

Football was Marcus's favourite thing in the world, and with every kick and touch, he was working towards his Manchester United dream.

Just like his new hero, Cristiano – who on first arriving in England in 2003, had played for himself with all those fancy flicks and tricks. But five years later, he was playing for the team instead. His mind was focused on glory, and growing numbers:

Goals per season – 9, 12, 23!

Assists per season – 10, 9, 21!

Trophies – one FA Cup, one League Cup, two Premier League titles…

…and one Champions League?

Manchester United were through to the semi-finals of the 2007–08 tournament, and Marcus, like most United fans, was dreaming of European glory. He had only been two years old when the team won it in 1999, so this one would be extra special for him.

Come On You Reds!

UNI-TED! UNI-TED!

Five years on from the Brazilian Ronaldo's hat-trick hero performance, Marcus was back at Old Trafford to watch another big Champions League night. This time, United were up against the other

Spanish giants, Barcelona, and it was 0–0 going into the second leg. So no away goals scored, but none conceded either.

Come On You Reds!

UNI-TED! UNI-TED!

As the game kicked off, the atmosphere in the stadium was like nothing that Marcus had ever experienced before. It was as if the noise and passion of the fans was a physical force, pushing the United players forward, up the pitch, towards that final...

In the fourteenth minute, the new Ronaldo, Cristiano, dribbled at the Barcelona defence, weaving one way and then the other.

'Go on, go on!' Marcus urged his favourite trickster.

Gianluca Zambrotta did stop Cristiano eventually, but his clearance fell straight to Scholesy, who took one touch and then fired a wonderstrike into the top corner. 1–0 to United!

As the ball hit the back of the net, Old Trafford roared and rocked like it might fall down.

'Come on!' screamed Scholesy, down on the pitch.

And 'Come on!' screamed Marcus, up in the stands.

What a start! The next seventy-six minutes, however, were some of the most nerve-wracking and nail-biting of Marcus's young football life.

Edwin van der Sar saved from Lionel Messi. Yessss!

Ji-sung Park's shot went just wide. Noooo!

Carlos Tevez got past the Barcelona defence, but not past Víctor Valdés in goal. Noooo!

Van der Sar held on to Thierry Henry's header. Yessss!

Marcus kept looking up at the scoreboard, urging the seconds to pass. Surely, it was time for the referee to blow his whistle? At last, Rio Ferdinand headed the ball away to Tevez, who booted it up field... FWEEEEET – it was over!

'Yes, yes, YES!' Marcus yelled, hugging his brothers and anyone else he could find. What a victory – their team was through to another Champions League final!

It was a night that Marcus would never, ever forget. Those exciting European wins were why he was a Manchester United fan, and why one day, he was going to become a Manchester United hero too. Because if it felt that good just being a supporter, how good would it feel to be a player out there at the heart of the action?

Unbelievable – that was the answer! Marcus didn't really need any extra motivation, but it didn't hurt.

Three weeks later, things got even better. In the final in Moscow, United beat Chelsea 6–5 on penalties. It was another nail-biter for Marcus and his family but at least the right team had won in the end.

'Campeones, Campeones, Olé! Olé! Olé!' Marcus celebrated at home with his family.

United were the Champions of Europe, as well as the Champions of England! Marcus felt so proud to be a part of the club, and hopefully, its bright future. He vowed that, after Rooney and Ronaldo, there would be Rashford.

CHAPTER 8

GROWING UP FAST

One day at school, Marcus was asked to write about his dreams for the future. 'Easy!' he thought, picking up his pen. This was his favourite kind of classwork.

'I have one aim in life and that is to be a professional footballer, and hopefully at Manchester United.'

That was it; he wanted to make his family proud and make Old Trafford roar and rock.

As Marcus looked down at the words he'd written on the page, his goal suddenly seemed so simple. But actually, it was anything but simple. He was just one of millions of football-mad kids all over the world with exactly the same aim.

Marcus, however, had two key strengths

that helped him to stand out from the crowd at Manchester United:

1) talent

and

2) determination

As he progressed through the club's academy, Marcus stayed humble and Marcus stayed hungry. Whether it was free kicks or his left foot, there was always something that he wanted to improve, something that he wanted to work hard on.

'Come on, time to go home, lad,' the United youth coaches would tell him. 'We can practise that again next week.'

It was Marcus's attitude that impressed the club the most. That was why they decided to make him their youngest ever Schoolboy Scholar, at the age of just eleven.

'Wow, thanks!' was Marcus's first reaction when the coaches told him, but that was before he started thinking. Wait a second – what did becoming a 'Schoolboy Scholar' actually mean?

Well, the good news was that Marcus would get to

play a lot more football, even during school-time.

'Great, I'm in!'

But the bad news was that, in order to become a Manchester United Schoolboy Scholar, he would have to move schools and, more significantly, move away from home.

'Why?' he asked in surprise. He was only eleven! 'We don't live that far away, and Dwaine can just drive me there every day!'

Marcus wasn't sure that he was ready to leave his friends and family behind. Who would he have a kickaround with now? Where would he live – with strangers? And would he have to cook his own meals?

'No, there's a nice lady called Maria,' his mum explained, 'who has looked after lots of young Manchester United stars. You would be living with her, but don't worry, we will still see you all the time!'

Okay – if that's what it would take to achieve his one aim in life, then Marcus would do it. He was determined.

'Are you sure this is what you want?' his mum asked, as they arrived at Maria's house for a visit.

It was a big decision and Melanie couldn't help worrying about her little boy. After all, he was incredibly young to be away from home. But if this was what Marcus really wanted, then she wouldn't stand in his way.

By the end of the visit, she did feel a bit better about things. Maria was kind and friendly, telling stories about other Manchester United stars as she gave them a tour of the house.

'Gerard Piqué – yes, he could cause a bit of trouble, but bless him, he's a good boy really. He's gone back to Barcelona now, I hear…'

And for Melanie, it was also nice to know that her son wouldn't be staying there alone. There was another academy star living there too, another tricky winger in fact, called Tom Lawrence. He was three years older than Marcus, but they seemed to get on well straight away.

'Stick with me, mate,' Tom told him with a smile, 'and you'll be playing with the big boys in no time!'

Marcus loved the sound of that. Growing up with two big brothers, he was used to challenging himself against older, stronger, better players. And at the United academy, there were lots of those, especially in the Under-18s team.

Paul Pogba was a tall, talented midfielder from France,

Ravel Morrison was one of the most skilful players that Marcus had ever seen,

and Jesse Lingard was a lively little midfielder with an eye for goal.

Despite the big age difference, Marcus became friends with them. He was mature beyond his years and he wasn't afraid to introduce himself.

'Hi, is it true you used to play for Fletcher Moss?' he asked confidently.

Jesse smiled. 'Yeah, but only for a bit.'

'Cool, me too!' Marcus replied proudly.

It wasn't long until Manchester United's big boys were inviting him to join them in 'The Cage'. That's what they called their exciting freestyle football matches at the club's training centre in Carrington.

Paul McGuinness, their youth coach, thought it was a great idea.

'Just go a bit easy on him, okay?' he warned the older players. 'Remember – he's only twelve!'

McGuinness had a different message for Marcus, though. 'Show them what you can do, kid!' he said with a cheeky wink.

Sometimes, 'The Cage' was 11 vs 11, or even 13 vs 13, with chaos everywhere, and no space to take your time and think. Everything had to be done at super-speed – the skills, the shots, and most of all, the decision-making. Otherwise...

'Too late!' McGuinness would shout from the sideline. 'You need to play that pass earlier there, kid!'

'Yes, Coach!' Marcus would shout back, chasing after the ball again.

He was learning so much, with every minute that he played on the pitch. United's youngest-ever Schoolboy Scholar was growing up fast.

Sometimes, 'The Cage' was 7 vs 7, or 8 vs 8, which Marcus found way more fun. In those games, he had the time and space to really express himself, especially alongside such talented teammates. They made everything look so easy.

'Yes!' Paul called out for the ball.

As he played the pass, Marcus was already on the run again, demanding the ball back: 'One-two!'

When it arrived, he skipped past one tackle with a Ronaldo drop of the shoulder, then played another one-two with Paul. From the edge of the 'D', Marcus fired a fierce, low shot into the bottom corner. *GOAL!*

'Yes, mate!' Paul cheered as they celebrated with their special handshake.

On the sidelines, McGuinness clapped and smiled. The future of Manchester United looked very bright indeed.

CHAPTER 9

SIZE, STRENGTH AND SPEED

While Marcus seemed to be on a fast track to the top, he knew that in football, everything can change in an instant. One day, you could be the next big thing and a few weeks later, you could be the next one out the door. Marcus had seen it before. Between the ages of twelve and fourteen, many of his friends had left the Manchester United academy, for all kinds of reasons:

Too small,

Too slow,

Bad attitude,

Just not quite talented enough.

'Good luck!' they told him, moving on with no hard feelings.

For Marcus, it was always sad to say goodbye to teammates that he had played with for years. And it was also worrying – what if he was the next one to go?

But still, Marcus was determined to stay and become a Manchester United hero, even if that dream was starting to look more and more difficult. No-one doubted that he had the skill to succeed, and the willpower too, but what about the size, the strength and the speed?

Speed? Yes, speed! Before, Marcus had been one of the fastest players in the United youth team, but when his legs began to grow, his body struggled to keep up. As it tried to adapt, there was pain and there were problems slowing him down. Suddenly, he couldn't glide gracefully past defenders anymore. But why not? What was going on? It was like he had lost his football superpower.

'My career is over!' Marcus moaned dramatically as he trudged off the pitch after another frustrating performance. He was finding it hard to get into the game, and when he did, none of his skills seemed to work as well as they used to.

There was no way that he was going to become a top winger at United if he didn't retain his blistering pace. Perhaps he would have to move to a different position on the pitch, a position where speed wasn't so important. Maybe he could become a central midfielder instead, using his creativity and football brain...

No, no, no – United's youth coaches weren't going to let that happen. They knew that Marcus was made to attack.

'Hey, don't worry about your pace at the moment, kid,' the Under-16s boss, Neil Ryan, said, trying to lift his spirits. He had coached so many boys with growing pains before and he knew that the bad times wouldn't last. 'You'll get your speed back soon, I promise, but first, we need to work on your strength.'

Marcus certainly had the mental strength, but not the physical strength yet. Without that, he would never get his burst of speed back and big defenders would keep knocking him off the ball too easily. So, it was time for him to build up his core strength in the gym.

Planks, stomach crunches, bridges, leg raises, sit-ups… It was long, hard, boring work, but luckily for Marcus, his teammate, Axel Tuanzebe, was there to turn everything into a competition.

'Right, first to fifty press-ups wins… GO!'

Axel was already a big, strong defender, but Marcus hated to lose at anything, even press-ups. So their rivalry pushed him to improve. Once he set himself a goal, he would keep working until he achieved it.

'Yes, I finally won!'

Throughout those difficult times, Marcus kept smiling and thinking positively about the future. There was no point moaning or giving up on his dream. He just had to get on with his gym work and pass this test. It was all part of the process, part of his journey to the Premier League.

When Marcus saw other academy stars making it into the Manchester United first team, it inspired him to keep going:

First, Federico Macheda,

Then Danny Welbeck,

Then Tom Cleverley,

And then in 2011, Marcus's mates from 'The Cage' – Paul, Ravel and Jesse.

If they could all do it, then so could he!

Marcus also found extra motivation at the 'Theatre of Dreams'. He was there watching in the Old Trafford crowd when Dimitar Berbatov scored a heroic hat-trick to beat Liverpool 3–2, and when Rooney scored a brilliant bicycle-kick to win the Manchester derby against City.

'That's going to be me one day!' Marcus kept telling himself. That's what he was working towards, and it would all be worth it. He could do this; things were going to get better. Size, strength and speed – he would need all three to become a superstar like his United heroes.

'That's it, kid,' Ryan encouraged him. 'Keep battling for that ball!'

Marcus was a young man on a mission. Day after day, he got a little bit bigger, a little bit stronger, and a little bit faster again.

Just after his fifteenth birthday, he got his first England call-up, to play for the Under-16s in the Victory Shield against Wales. Next to Dominic Solanke and Joe Gomez, Marcus looked so tiny, but he didn't let that stop him.

'Well done, kid!' Kenny Swain, the manager, congratulated him after a brave and battling performance. Even on a tough night, Marcus had still shown moments of magic, moving so beautifully with the ball. It was easy to see the boy's huge potential, but he still had some developing to do.

By the time he turned sixteen, Marcus had also experienced his first taste of training with the United first team. What an amazing experience it was, to be up close and personal with proper Premier League stars! He barely touched the ball all session, but that didn't matter. What mattered was that he was making progress.

He was far from being the finished footballer yet, but his youth coaches weren't worried about that. They now knew that he had the hunger and determination to overcome any setback. The rest could wait. The club was happy to be patient with Marcus as his body grew, because this was a boy who was destined for Manchester United greatness.

CHAPTER 10

FROM NUMBER 10 TO NUMBER 9

Yes, Marcus was destined for Manchester United greatness, but what position would he play? After starting out on the right wing, the academy had moved him all over the attack: left wing, striker, Number 10. So, where would he play his best football?

That was the hot topic amongst the club's youth coaches. They'd had a similar problem a few years earlier with another ex-Fletcher Moss forward: Danny Welbeck. Was he a winger or was he a striker? In the end, they left it too late to decide and they didn't want to make the same mistake with Marcus.

'The kid's got too much talent to just stay up front and shoot,' some argued. 'That's not his style. He wants to be on the ball all the time!'

That was true; Marcus was really enjoying life in the Number 10 playmaker role. Buzzing around behind a striker, he had a lot more space and time to use his number one weapon: skills!

But not all of his coaches saw it that way: 'No, he looks like a classic modern striker to me. He's fast, he's going to be at least six feet tall and he can dribble with the ball too. Surely, he's more Thierry Henry than David Silva, isn't he? There's only one thing missing at the moment – goals.'

Marcus did score goals for the United Under-16s, but to become a top Number 9, he would need to start scoring a lot more often. So it was time for some special striker lessons.

'Instead of dropping deep to collect the ball, we want you racing in behind the defence,' the Under-18s coach, Colin Little, taught him in training. 'It's all about getting yourself in the right position, and then timing your run to perfection. Let's give it a go.'

Marcus loved learning new things, especially when it came to football. So, he practised bursting into the box again and again, from every angle.

'Yes!' he called out, pointing forward to where he wanted the pass to go.

'That's better!' Little encouraged him. 'If you're sprinting onto a through-ball at top speed, no centre-back in the world is going to catch you.'

That was only the first part of the striking process, though. Once Marcus had the ball on the half-turn, he had to learn to be lethal. *TOUCH, BANG!.. GOAL!*

'Don't over-think it when you're in those positions,' Little told him. 'It's all about instinct and finding your rhythm. Just picture the goal, pick your spot and SHOOT!'

Marcus wasn't a natural finisher like van Nistelrooy, but he was always willing to work hard to improve. He read all the guides that his coaches gave him and then asked them lots of questions.

'So, let's say Dev is dribbling down the wing. Should I make a run to the near post, or between the centre-backs?'

'If Axel is looking to play a long ball out from the back, should I move out wide into the channels, or stay in the middle and try to win the flick-on for Callum?'

McGuinness and Little were delighted to see their young star taking striking so seriously.

Marcus also watched hours and hours of highlights from the best strikers in the business: Sergio Agüero at Manchester City, Luis Suárez at Liverpool, and of course, his old United hero, Cristiano Ronaldo at Real Madrid. Just like Marcus, Ronaldo had started out as a skilful playmaker, but he had turned himself into a super striker instead. He had just scored sixty goals in a single season!

Marcus could only dream of getting that many, but it was great to see Cristiano combining skills with goals. Maybe he would enjoy being a top striker, after all! Soon, it was time for him to put his lessons into practice on the pitch. Could Marcus shine as Manchester United's new Number 9?

At the start of the 2014–15 season, his youth coaches made a wise decision. They kept him in the Under-18s squad, rather than sending him up into the Reserves.

He was ready to play at a higher level, but there was no rush for him to compete against big, bruising defenders. Why not let him build up his confidence first, against smaller, less experienced centre-backs?

It took him a few games to get going, but eventually Marcus found his scoring form in the Under-18 Premier League. He finished the season with thirteen goals in twenty-five starts.

'He's really starting to look like a striker now!' McGuinness and Little agreed excitedly.

At the Mercedes-Benz Junior Cup in Berlin, Marcus scored two goals, plus a penalty in the final shoot-out, as Manchester United lifted the trophy.

'Hurraaaaaaaay!'

In the 2015 UEFA Youth League, the coach, Nicky Butt, made Marcus captain. In his first game against PSV Eindhoven, he scored a penalty and then burst into the box to convert Tyler Reid's cross. *One game, two goals!*

And what about the FA Youth Cup? The Class of '92 had won the competition, and so had Paul, Ravel and Jesse in 2011.

Marcus knew that it was the perfect place to make a name for himself. He scored a stunning free kick against Tottenham during his first tournament, and he was an even better striker second time around.

As Callum Whelan collected the ball just inside the QPR half, Marcus was already on the move, between the centre-backs.

'Yes!' he called out, pointing forward to where he wanted the pass to go.

Marcus was through, one on one with the keeper, but as he dropped his shoulder and dribbled around him, the keeper clipped his legs. Penalty!

Marcus picked himself up, and then rushed over to pick up the ball. That spot-kick was his. He was United's Number 9 now, and he was going to score. After a slow run-up, he blasted the ball into the back of the net.

Goooooooooooooooooooooaaaaaaaaaaaaaaaallllllllllllll llllllllllllllll!!!!!!!!!!!!!!!!!!!!!

'Get in!' Marcus was really starting to love that scoring feeling. And with every strike, he was getting closer and closer to his target – the Manchester United first team.

CHAPTER 11

DREAM DEBUT 1

'Today, we had Marcus Rashford on the bench,' Manchester United manager Louis van Gaal told the media after their Premier League match against Watford in November 2015. 'He's a fantastic talent.'

Wow, what a wonderful thing to hear! Marcus didn't make it onto the pitch that time, but still, he got to sit with Sergio Romero, Marcos Rojo and Andreas Pereira on the bench. And best of all, he had his own squad number now – 39. It even had a '9' in it!

That season, United were really struggling for fit strikers. They still had Wayne Rooney, plus Anthony Martial and youngsters James Wilson and Will

Keane, but they were often out ill or injured. So, who else could they call on?

'Me, me – pick me!' Marcus tried to show his manager whenever he got the chance to train with the first team.

After all, van Gaal was famous for giving young players a chance. He had handed Clarence Seedorf, Patrick Kluivert and Edgar Davids their debuts at Ajax, then Xavi, Andrés Iniesta, Carles Puyol and Víctor Valdés their debuts at Barcelona. The Dutchman clearly had a good eye for spotting future superstars, so who had impressed him at Manchester United so far?

The club's youngsters found out the answer in February 2016, when Wayne, James and Will all had to miss United's Europa League second leg against FC Midtjylland. Anthony would start up front, with Jesse and Memphis Depay on the wings, but they'd need some back-up on the bench. So van Gaal decided to include his favourite young striker in the squad.

'Mum, I'm in – I made it!' Marcus shouted proudly into his phone.

He couldn't believe it – what an incredible opportunity for an eighteen-year-old! United were 2–1 down after the first leg in Denmark, so there was a good chance that, in this second leg, Marcus might be needed to help attack later in the second half.

In fact, he was needed a whole lot sooner than that. As the squad warmed up at Old Trafford, one United player pulled up with an injury. It was Anthony. Uh oh, what were they going to do without their top goal scorer? Move Memphis up front and then Juan Mata to the left wing? No, van Gaal wanted to play with a proper striker.

'Rashford, get ready – you're starting!'

Starting? For the Manchester United first team? At Old Trafford? Oh boy, this was *BIG!* It was a good thing that Marcus didn't have much time to think about it. Kick-off was only minutes away.

'Just play your natural game tonight,' van Gaal instructed him. 'Express yourself – show the world what you can do.'

'Mate, you're gonna be great!' Jesse told him in the tunnel.

Marcus nodded. He was a little nervous, of course, but mostly excited. His childhood goal was about to come true. They didn't call it the 'Theatre of Dreams' for nothing! All those striking lessons with Little, all those goals for the Under-18s – they were preparing him for this massive moment. He just had to stay calm out there and make the most of any opportunities that came his way.

'Marcus who?' some of the United supporters asked each other when they saw the final team sheet. But they soon knew all about their new star striker.

In the fifteenth minute, Morgan Schneiderlin dribbled into the Midtjylland box.

'Yes!' Marcus yelled to his left, not afraid to call for the ball. He took one touch to control it, and then thought about the shot straight away. His strike was powerful and on target, but a defender blocked it.

'Good effort!' his United teammates encouraged him. 'Keep going, kid!'

With Old Trafford urging him on, Marcus never stopped moving. Sometimes, he appeared on the left, sometimes on the right, and sometimes in the middle. Midtjylland had no idea how to mark him! When his team had possession, Marcus ran into space to make himself available for the pass. And when they didn't, he chased after the defenders to win the ball back. He wanted it all the time.

From a throw-in, Marcus turned and attacked the penalty area at speed. With a left-foot stepover, he made space for the shot... *BANG!* The ball was travelling towards the bottom corner, but the keeper dived down to push it wide.

'Unlucky!' he heard Jesse clap and cheer.

Marcus was getting closer and closer to a debut goal. He could feel his confidence growing with every touch. He was playing with freedom, like he was just in the park with his mates. He even dared to do a cheeky backheel one-two with Juan. The United fans roared with delight. They loved him already! The tricks didn't always come off, but at least Marcus was brave enough to try.

It was 1–1 at half-time, meaning 3–2 to Midtjylland on aggregate. United needed goals in the second half, and soon.

A cross from the right flew over Memphis's head, but Juan just managed to keep it in. He cut the ball back to the edge of the six-yard box, which seemed to be empty… but wait! Marcus had the speed of thought and the speed of foot to get there in a flash. With a cool side-foot, he passed the ball into the net. 3–3!

Gooooooooooooooooooooaaaaaaaaaaaaaaaallllllllllll lllllllllllllll!!!!!!!!!!!!!!!!!!!!!

Old Trafford was rocking, and it was all because of Marcus. What a feeling – words couldn't describe it! He raced over to the corner flag and into the arms of the celebrating fans. Only a few weeks earlier, he had been a Manchester United supporter, just like them. Now, he was also a Manchester United scorer.

'Great stuff, Rash,' the captain, Michael Carrick, congratulated him. 'Right lads, let's get another goal!'

And who was most likely to score it? Marcus, of course. Every time he touched the ball he looked so dangerous.

As Guillermo Varela looked up to cross it in from the right, he saw Marcus with his arm up, waiting in space near the penalty spot. United's Number

39 followed the flight of the ball carefully and then placed his shot past the keeper. 4–3!

Goooooooooooooooooooooaaaaaaaaaaaaaaaaaallllllllllll llllllllllllllll!!!!!!!!!!!!!!!!!!!!

Marcus ran over to celebrate with the same supporters again. What a night! Was this really happening? He had imagined his Manchester United debut many times before, but this was way beyond even his wildest dreams.

It was a very special, proud moment, not just for Marcus, but also for his friends, family and for all the coaches who had helped him along the way, from Fletcher Moss Rangers and then through the United youth teams – Gaynord, Horrocks, McGuinness, Ryan, Little. They had all believed in the little boy wonder, and just look at him now!

Although he couldn't quite complete his hat-trick, Marcus was undoubtedly the man of the match. A new United hero had been born – and all because of an injury in the warm-up.

CHAPTER 12

DREAM DEBUT 2

The days of 'Marcus who?' were over. Suddenly, everyone was talking about the eighteen-year-old striker who had just bagged two goals on his Manchester United debut. He was now the club's youngest-ever scorer in Europe, beating the great George Best's record. And it wasn't just the goals; it was also the skill, the speed, the style, the energy. Marcus had already created a buzz of excitement.

So what next for United's new young star? With the pressure on, would he prove to be a one-game wonder like Macheda, or was he the real deal?

It didn't take long for the fans to find out. With United's injury crisis continuing, three days later,

Marcus found himself once again in the starting line-up. This time, he would be making his Premier League debut, against Arsenal. Wow, it was a good thing that he was such a cool, calm character.

'More of the same, yeah Rash?' Jesse joked in the dressing room before kick-off.

Marcus smiled back confidently, 'I'll see what I can do, mate!'

He tried to stay relaxed for as long as possible, but once he heard the passion of the fans and felt his feet touch that Old Trafford pitch, his mind was fully focused. Focused on winning, and hopefully, scoring some more goals.

Come On You Reds!
UNI-TED! UNI-TED!

Right from kick-off, United were the team on top, and once again, their new Number 39 was the player to watch. The Arsenal defence just could not cope with Marcus's speed and movement. When he got the ball and burst between two of them, all they could do was bring him down. *Free kick, just outside the box!*

'That's it, mate!' Memphis shouted. 'Keep running at them – they're scared of you!'

Marcus nodded – dribbling at defenders was what he loved best. But he wasn't all about skills anymore; he was also a goal scorer now. So if Arsenal switched off for even a second, he was ready to pounce like a proper Premier League striker…

In the twenty-ninth minute, Gabriel Paulista got to Guillermo's cross first, but the Arsenal defender couldn't clear it properly. In fact, he passed it straight to Marcus, who had stolen in at the back post. He didn't even take a touch to control it. In a flash, he curled a powerful shot past the keeper and into the top corner. 1–0!

Goooooooooooooooooooooaaaaaaaaaaaaaaaaaalllllllllllll llllllllllllll!!!!!!!!!!!!!!!!!!

That amazing adrenaline rush again.

'Yes, you hero!' Juan screamed, throwing his arm around Marcus as they ran together towards the corner flag. He was certainly part of the team now.

'What a life-changing three days for Marcus Rashford!' the TV commentator cried out.

Two goals on his United debut, and now one on his Premier League debut too – Marcus was on fire! As he leapt into the air in front of the fans, he didn't think that life could get any better.

But there was more to come. Three minutes later, Jesse chipped a dangerous ball into the Arsenal box, aiming for United's new star striker. Marcus had positioned himself perfectly, just like Little had taught him: in between the centre-backs.

'Go on, kid!' the fans urged, growing more and more excited in their seats.

Marcus still had plenty of work to do, though.

He wasn't the tallest of strikers, but he timed his jump brilliantly, keeping his eyes on the ball floating towards him.

Jesse's cross didn't have that much power on it, but Marcus used his neck muscles to swing his head around and nod it down into the bottom corner. *2–0!*

Goooooooooooooooooooooaaaaaaaaaaaaaaaallllllllllll llllllllllllll!!!!!!!!!!!!!!!!!!

'You couldn't make this up,' the commentator cried out again in utter disbelief. 'This is truly astonishing!'

'Thanks, mate!' Marcus yelled, racing over to give Jesse a big hug. After scoring all those goals together in 'The Cage' when they were younger, they knew each other well, but it was a dream come true to now be doing it at Old Trafford, and for the first team.

Two games, four goals – and still, United's new star striker wasn't finished. He kept running and fighting and calling for the ball. He wasn't playing for himself; he was playing for his team.

When Arsenal's attacker Mesut Özil whipped the ball into the box, it was Marcus who was back there to clear it away.

And when their keeper Petr Čech received a back pass, it was Marcus who rushed forward to close him down.

Later in the second half, when Marcus found three Arsenal defenders blocking his path in the penalty area, he didn't try to trick his way through. Instead, he took his time, looked up and spotted Ander Herrera running forward, calling for the pass. 3–1!

'Thanks, Rash!' Ander yelled as the United players all celebrated together.

After two goals and one assist in eighty magical minutes, Marcus's day was done. As he walked slowly off the field, every United supporter was up on their feet, applauding and chanting his name.

Rashford! Rashford! Rashford!

It was a very emotional moment for Marcus, but just like when he got the ball in front of goal, he looked so cool about it. Nothing fazed him at all. He just calmly climbed the steps to the subs bench, handing out high-fives on the way to his seat.

Pressure? What pressure? Marcus was loving life in the Manchester United first team. He had the self-belief, and also the talent to back it up.

'In my experience, youngsters often play well in their first match,' van Gaal said afterwards, 'but the second is different. Marcus did well in his second match, so he's a special talent, I think.'

It was clear to van Gaal that Marcus had already proved himself; surely now it was easy for everyone else to see that he was definitely the real deal.

CHAPTER 13

MANCHESTER DERBY MAGIC

After his two dream debuts, Marcus's next games for Manchester United were underwhelming. His next five games for the club passed without him scoring a single goal. Oh dear, was the kid going to be a two-game wonder, after all?

Of course not! Although he was disappointed, Marcus didn't let his head drop. He kept working hard in training and listening to the older teammates around him.

'Don't worry. At your age, you're going to have good days and bad days,' Wayne Rooney reassured him. 'I definitely did, anyway!'

Marcus was glad to hear that, especially from a

United legend and one of his childhood heroes. Wayne knew exactly what it felt like to be the 'next big thing' in English football – all of the hype and the pressure. He had only been sixteen when he scored that wondergoal for Everton against Arsenal.

'You've just got to ignore all the talk and stay focused on your football,' Wayne continued. 'That's my advice, not that you need it. You're gonna be great!'

When the day of the Manchester derby arrived, Wayne was still out injured. That meant another start for Marcus in attack, less than a month after his club debut. This time, he had to score. He couldn't go SIX games without a goal – he was meant to be United's new star striker!

As he prepared for the big game, Marcus watched the video of Wayne's brilliant, derby-winning bicycle-kick, from back in 2011. He had been there in the Old Trafford crowd to witness that amazing moment. Now, five years later, it was Marcus's turn to try and become a Manchester derby hero.

'Come on, I can do this!' he kept telling himself.

A lot had changed since 2011, however. City were now two-time Premier League Champions and their team was packed with talent. Sergio Agüero, David Silva, Jesús Navas, Raheem Sterling, Yaya Touré – they had an experienced attack worth millions and millions!

The United attack, on the other hand, was all about youth and potential. Jesse was twenty-three, Anthony was twenty and Marcus was eighteen. They hadn't even played fifty Premier League games between them! So, what could they achieve together, away at the Etihad Stadium?

For the first fifteen minutes, Marcus mostly watched from the halfway line as City attacked again and again. Navas fired his first shot wide and then his second straight at David de Gea.

'Focus!' The United keeper clapped and cheered as he organised his teammates to defend the corner-kick.

Marcus could already tell that he wasn't going to get many chances to score that afternoon. Oh well, that just meant that he would have to be a more clinical striker.

And a smarter striker too. He wasn't having much luck on the left against the pace and power of Eliaquim Mangala and Gaël Clichy, so Marcus switched to the other side.

At last, United brought the ball forward, out of their own half. As Morgan Schneiderlin passed it through to Juan, Marcus positioned himself between City's other two defenders: centre-back Martín Demichelis and right-back Bacary Sagna.

This was a key part of United's game plan. If Marcus could just get himself one-on-one with Demichelis, he knew that he could destroy the Argentinian with his speed and skill. The plan had nearly worked the first time, and now Marcus was ready to try again.

Anthony made the run down the wing, to drag Sagna out wide. This was it – United's best opportunity to score.

'Yes!' Marcus called out for the ball. He was feeling even more confident now. It was time to show off those fast feet with a moment of Manchester derby magic.

With his first touch, he controlled it,

With his second, he attacked,

And with his third, he slid the ball through Demichelis' legs.

NUTMEG! Marcus was through, one on one with Joe Hart.

'Go on, go on, go on!' the United fans urged, jumping to their feet.

The pressure was on, but Marcus didn't panic. He wasn't going to waste this huge chance. Everything seemed to slow down around him, but he was in the zone, in total control of the situation. He took his time, picked his spot and then slotted the ball past the City keeper. *1–0!*

Gooooooooooooooooooooaaaaaaaaaaaaaaaaalllllllllllll llllllllllllll!!!!!!!!!!!!!!!!!!!

What a cool, calm finish in his first-ever Manchester derby! It was his new favourite goal *EVER*.

'Yesssssssssss!' Marcus was bursting with pride as he raced into Anthony's arms. He had done it – he had scored a goal against their greatest rivals, City! Soon, he had Jesse jumping on his back too.

'Mate, that was ice-cold!'

Marcus had scored on his United debut, then on his Premier League debut, and now on his Manchester derby debut. He was a big game player, that was for sure.

The next seventy-five minutes were long and nervy for United, but at least Marcus was out there playing on the pitch, rather than watching from the stands. Could he grab a second goal to make things more comfortable?

Before half-time, Marcus ran onto Morgan's flick and tried to dribble past Demichelis again. Just as he was about to skip past him, the defender cut across him and clipped his legs.

'Penalty!' Marcus cried out as he fell to the floor, and so did every other United player and supporter in the stadium.

The referee, however, shook his head. What?! As Marcus got back up, the City defenders surrounded him, accusing him of diving.

'No way!' he defended himself fiercely. Cheating wasn't his style. 'I'm not a diver!'

The City players were trying to make Marcus lose his temper, but he wasn't falling for that. By the time the game restarted, he was calm and focused again. No problem, he would find another way to win the game for United.

He kept dribbling at Demichelis until eventually City had to take him off early in the second half. It was safer that way; Marcus was causing him too many problems.

United's Number 39 was tireless and fearless; even when Marcus got cramp, he carried on fighting for his team. In the last seconds of the match, he dribbled the ball forward from deep in his own half, all the way up to the corner flag. Mangala did tackle him in the end, but his run had relieved the pressure on the United defence and wasted some valuable time.

'Great work, Rash!' Jesse called out when he caught up with him at last.

At the final whistle, Marcus was exhausted, but also emotional. What a day! He shook his head in disbelief. Unbelievable! The last thing he needed was Jesse jumping on his back again, screaming in his ear:

'Mate, we did it! We won The Derby – Manchester is RED thanks to you!'

Others might have become arrogant at that moment, but not Marcus. He stayed humble and hungry. The next day, he was back at school as normal, studying for his BTEC, as if he hadn't done anything special at all.

CHAPTER 14

TROPHY TIME

Two goals on his United debut, two more on his Premier League debut and now the winner in the Manchester derby – could Marcus's breakthrough season get any better?

Yes, if he could win a team trophy! Wasn't that what every player wanted most of all? United were already out of the League Cup and the Europa League, plus they were down in sixth place in the Premier League. So the only competition left was the FA Cup, which they hadn't lifted for twelve years.

'Come on, let's make that trophy ours!' said the captain, Michael, urging on his teammates. As a club legend, he was used to winning lots of silverware.

United's chances of lifting the FA Cup were looking good until they drew 1–1 with West Ham at Old Trafford in the sixth round. Now, they would need to win the replay at the Boleyn Ground. That didn't sound too difficult, but other than that famous Manchester derby victory, United's away form was awful. Still, with Marcus, Anthony and Jesse all there in attack, anything could happen...

Early in the second half, Anthony burst forward with the ball and slipped it through to Marcus on the edge of the West Ham box. DANGER ALERT! He had one defender in front of him and three more chasing from behind, but Marcus had been practising his best Brazilian Ronaldo impression for years.

Tap, stepover to the left, shift to the right...
BANG! – TOP CORNER!

Gooooooooooooooooooooaaaaaaaaaaaaaaaalllllllllllll
llllllllllllll!!!!!!!!!!!!!!!!!!!!

'Mate, what a strike!' Anthony congratulated Marcus with a high-five and a hug.

Together, they were forming a very promising strike partnership, with so much pace and skill.

It was Anthony who grabbed the winner against Everton in the semis to take United through to the FA Cup Final.

'Get in!' Marcus cheered loudly as the team celebrated in front of the fans at Wembley.

A month later, United were back there at 'The Home of Football' to take on Crystal Palace, and hopefully, to end their season on a high.

For Marcus, it was his first taste of that special Wembley Cup final atmosphere. Wow, what an experience! As the two teams walked out onto the field, they came face-to-face with the sights and sounds of 88,000 supporters.

Come On You Reds!

We all Follow the Palace!

UNI-TED! UNI-TED!

EAG-LES! EAG-LES!

Marcus had already played in the Manchester derby, in European nights at Old Trafford and also away at Anfield, but this felt even bigger. That's because there was a top trophy up for grabs. Winning the FA Cup would be the perfect way to end his exciting first season at United. 'Eighteen games, eight goals and one trophy' – yes, that sounded so much better.

So Marcus started the 2016 FA Cup Final like a hero in a hurry. After a clever one-two with Wayne, he dribbled all the way down the left wing and into the Palace penalty area. He almost escaped past Damien Delaney, but at the last second, the defender cleared the ball out for a corner.

'Come on!' the United fans roared, feeding off the energy of their young striker.

Soon, he was at it again, this time on the right wing. With a clever dummy, Marcus skipped straight past Delaney at the second attempt. As he carried the ball forward, he looked up and spotted Anthony running in at the back post. The cross was good, but the shot was bravely blocked.

'Unlucky!' Michael clapped and cheered from midfield. 'Keep going!'

Unfortunately, those were Manchester United's best moments in a poor first half. They were struggling to find a way past the strong Palace defence. It was going to take a moment of magic, and Marcus looked the most likely player to create it. He felt confident enough to try his full range of tricks, even in a big Wembley final.

Early in the second half, Marcus thought he'd finally managed it. With a classy flick, he slipped the ball through to Marouane Fellaini, who struck it fiercely first time towards the top corner... *BACK OFF THE RIGHT POST!*

'Ohhhhhhhh!' Marcus groaned along with 50,000 others.

Eight minutes later, Anthony's glancing header flew towards the bottom corner... *BACK OFF THE LEFT POST!*

So close again! And that was as close as United got to a goal while Marcus was still on the pitch. In the seventy-third minute, he jumped up for a header and landed awkwardly.

'Argghh!' he cried out, clutching his right knee down on the grass.

Marcus was desperate to carry on playing, but he couldn't. The pain was just too intense. With a sad shake of the head, he hobbled off the pitch and straight down the tunnel to the dressing room.

What a disappointment, especially when he was playing so well in a cup final at Wembley! Five minutes later, things got even worse, when Palace took the lead. Nooooooo!

'Come on, United!' Marcus muttered under his breath as he lay there on the treatment table.

Luckily, his teammates fought back straight away. Marouane chested down Wayne's cross and Juan volleyed it in: 1–1 – back in the game!

The excitement and drama carried on in extra-time. When Chris Smalling was sent off, it didn't look good for United. But five minutes later, their super sub, Jesse, volleyed home the winning goal.

'Get in!' Although it was hard not joining in with the team celebrations, Marcus was so happy for his best mate. After the final whistle, he limped over in his team tracksuit for their special FA Cup Final handshake.

'Yes, JLingz – I knew you'd score today! The tekkers on that strike, eh?'

Together, they climbed the Wembley steps to collect their winners' medals. Then, after a short wait, it was trophy time for United.

'Hurraaaaaaaay!' the whole team cheered as Wayne and Michael lifted the FA Cup high above their heads.

What a day, what a season! Marcus still had to pinch himself sometimes, just to check that he wasn't dreaming. His breakthrough year at United felt too good to be true.

And hopefully, as long as his injury wasn't too serious, his sensational season wasn't over yet. Because even though Marcus hadn't made his England debut yet, the manager, Roy Hodgson, had just named him in his squad for Euro 2016.

CHAPTER 15

EURO 2016

When he first heard the news, Marcus couldn't
believe it. 'Me, going to Euro 2016 with England,
at the age of eighteen?' he thought to himself.
No way, someone must be playing a nasty joke on
him. One of his mates? One of his brothers?

But no, it was true, it was really happening! After
his amazing first half-season at United, Marcus was
about to become an England international, and maybe
play for his country at a top tournament. Unbelievable!

'It's mad – I haven't even played for the Under-
21s yet!' he told his family, shaking his head with
a mixture of disbelief and delight.

Ahead of Euro 2016, everyone knew England's

top three strikers: Wayne Rooney, Harry Kane and Jamie Vardy. However, in Hodgson's squad, there was space for four forwards, maybe even five.
So, the national team manager had some difficult decisions to make. Should he go for an experienced goal scorer like Jermain Defoe or Daniel Sturridge, or an exciting young maverick like Marcus?

England had a history of taking their best young attackers to major tournaments. Wayne had gone to his first one at the age of eighteen, as had Michael Owen and Alex Oxlade-Chamberlain, while Theo Walcott had been picked in the 2006 World Cup squad at the age of seventeen.

So why shouldn't Marcus be next at Euro 2016? Some argued that it was too soon for him, but others could see that he was ready to shine.

'I think Marcus Rashford will go to the Euros,' said former England striker, Ian Wright. 'He has pace, he makes super runs and he finishes comfortably: He's got everything.'

In the end, Hodgson selected Marcus and Daniel in his first squad of twenty-six, but England would only be able to take twenty-three players to the tournament. Three would be left behind, but who would they be?

Not Marcus! No, he was determined to impress his national team manager, both on the training field and also in the pre-tournament friendlies.

He didn't play in the 2–1 win over Turkey, but with Daniel injured, Marcus made his England debut against Australia at the Stadium of Light in Sunderland. Right, he thought, time to shine! In the second minute of the match, left-back Ryan Bertrand played the ball up to Marcus, who passed it over to Raheem Sterling on the wing.

'One-two!' Marcus called for it back, in space just inside the penalty area.

Raheem decided to go for the cross instead, but the ball bounced off the Australian defender and looped up in the air...

Marcus was onto it in a flash. As it dropped, he calmly volleyed it past the keeper. *1–0!*

Goooooooooooooaaaaaaaaaaaaallllllllllllllllll!!!!!!!!!!!!!

It was another debut goal for Marcus, and this time for his country. It was unreal – he hadn't even been on the field for three minutes! With his arms out wide, he raced over to the corner flag to celebrate.

'Mate, you've got that magic touch!' Raheem shouted, with a big smile on his face.

Marcus grinned back at his new teammate. Hopefully, Hodgson would see that too.

His dream England debut lasted sixty-three minutes, and before he was subbed off, he also helped set up the second goal for Wayne.

Jordan Henderson's pass was coming straight towards Marcus, but at the last second, he heard a shout from Raheem, who was racing up behind him. So with a drop of the shoulder, he dummied the ball and let it run through to Raheem, who crossed it to Wayne. 2–0!

It was high-fives all round for England's new attack. Surely, Marcus had to go to the Euros now?

'I'd take him,' his United captain, Michael, told the media. 'He brings something different.'

Marcus didn't play at all in their last friendly against Portugal, but when Hodgson selected his final England squad, his name was there on the list.

'Mum, I'm in!' he shouted down the phone. 'I made it – I'm going to France!'

Things were moving so fast for Marcus that he found it hard to take it all in. He had dreamed of playing at the 2018 World Cup and Euro 2020, but never Euro 2016.

'This is crazy!' he thought to himself, as he set off on his latest football adventure.

Marcus knew that he wouldn't be starting for England at the Euros, but hopefully he would at least get the chance to be a super sub once or twice.

He stayed on the bench for the first game against Russia, but in the second against Wales, England were drawing 1–1 with twenty minutes to go.

'Marcus, you're coming on!' one of the coaches called out.

Yes! He raced onto the pitch, ready to become England's super sub. In the end, however, it was Daniel who did that job instead, playing a one-two with Dele Alli and then poking the ball into the bottom corner. *2–1!*

As Marcus celebrated the goal with the others,

he couldn't help wishing that he had been the hero. Still, the main thing was that England were winning. He had to be a team player and wait his turn.

'Nice one, Studge!'

Having taken his chance against Wales, Daniel got to start the last group game, and the Round of 16 game against Iceland. Marcus, meanwhile, watched most of the match from the bench.

'Come on, England!'

After a confident start, the team totally collapsed. From 1–0 up, they went 2–1 down, and it was like the players had forgotten how to pass the ball. What was going on? If they didn't start playing properly soon, England were heading for a humiliating early exit.

For Marcus, it was so hard to just sit there and do nothing. He wanted to help turn things around, but instead he fidgeted on the bench while Hodgson brought on Jack Wilshere and then Jamie Vardy...

There were only five minutes left, when Marcus finally got the call. But that was still enough time for a few moments of magic. As soon as he got the ball, he raced up the left wing, past one defender and then another.

'Go on, go on!' the fans urged him on. It was now or never for England.

Marcus was into the Iceland box, with Harry Kane and Jamie Vardy waiting in the middle, but a defender slid in and poked the ball away.

'Come on!' Marcus wasn't giving up. He grabbed the ball and raced over to take the corner himself. In those last five minutes, he completed three dangerous dribbles, more than any of his teammates had managed during the rest of the match.

'Why wasn't Rashford on from the start?' the fans were left wondering. Unfortunately, it was all too little too late for England; they were heading home in disgrace.

So, would Marcus's experience at Euro 2016 affect his confidence? Not at all! Two months later, he made his debut for the Under-21s against Norway, and by the final whistle, he was an England hat-trick hero, walking off with the match-ball.

Marcus was simply unstoppable! And he was already looking ahead to the 2018 World Cup.

CHAPTER 16

LEARNING (FROM A LEGEND)

Back at Manchester United, there was great
excitement about the new 2016–17 season. They
not only had a new star manager – José Mourinho –
but also four new star signings:

Defender Eric Bailly,

Midfielder Henrikh Mkhitaryan,

Superstar striker Zlatan Ibrahimović,

And Paul Pogba. He was back! Yes, four years after
leaving to join Juventus, Marcus's old teammate from
'The Cage' had returned to Old Trafford.

'This is going to be so good!' Jesse predicted.

And Marcus agreed. Over the summer, he had
signed a brand-new contract, and moved from Number

39 to Number 19. He was making real progress, so he didn't mind about the extra competition in attack.

As much as he loved starting and scoring for United, Marcus knew that he wasn't ready to be the club's number-one striker. Not yet, anyway. That was too much pressure for an eighteen-year-old who had only recently broken into the first team. But now, with Zlatan there to partner Wayne and be the team's top goal scorer, Marcus had time to keep developing his game.

There was so much to learn from a legend like 'Ibra'. He was one of the best players of all time. Yes, he could seem a little too confident sometimes, but he had the talent and determination to back that up in the big games. He had scored goals everywhere – at Ajax, Juventus, Inter Milan, Barcelona, PSG – and had won tons of trophies too.

It was an amazing opportunity for Marcus to improve as a player and a striker. Each training session was like being back at school. He watched Zlatan as carefully as he could and tried to absorb as much information as possible.

It was Zlatan's mentality and focus that impressed Marcus the most. He had never met anyone who wanted to win as much as Zlatan did. Even in their 'friendly' matches during practice, he charged around the pitch, demanding the ball, and then barking angrily if he didn't get it. He was such a strong character that no-one messed with him, not even Mourinho!

If he ever missed a shot, Zlatan didn't let his head and shoulders drop. No – because he firmly believed that he would score the next one. And off the pitch, he worked so hard to keep himself fit and firing, even in his mid-thirties.

'That's what it takes to stay at the top level,' Zlatan told him one day. 'Especially when José is in charge!'

In the Manchester United first team matches, however, Marcus wasn't getting much game-time at all. He only came on as a second-half sub when United won the Community Shield, and he didn't play at all in their first two Premier League matches.

Oh dear, didn't Mourinho think he was good enough? A new manager was like a new start; Marcus would just have to prove himself all over again.

Away at Hull City, he came off the bench to score a last-minute winner. *GOAL!*

Away at Watford, he played a one-two with Zlatan and then bundled the ball in. *GOAL!*

At home against Leicester City, he converted Juan's cross. *GOAL!*

'That's more like it!' Marcus thought to himself as he raced over to the corner flag to celebrate. No matter what position Mourinho asked him to play, he was going to fight hard for his place in the team.

Marcus had switched from a winger to a striker in the United Under-18s, but now he was back out wide again. The United manager preferred to play Zlatan in the middle, with the other forwards taking it in turns on the wings. Marcus didn't mind, but it did mean that he had more defending to do.

'It's your job to mark the full-back,' Mourinho told him. 'When he goes forward, you track back!'

Sometimes Marcus was on the left and sometimes he was on the right. He had good games and not-so-good games, but they were all part of the learning process. He wasn't giving up or going out on loan; no, he would adapt, and he would succeed. Manchester United was his home and he was growing into a stronger all-round player.

Marcus's biggest problem during those difficult months was goals. From October 2016 through to April 2017, he went twenty Premier League games without scoring at all. The longer his bad run went on, the more people talked about it, and the more pressure he put on himself.

'Nooooo!' Marcus screamed at the sky as he wasted yet another simple chance. He could imagine the frustrated look on his manager's face.

What had happened to his finishing? If he didn't find his scoring touch again soon, Mourinho would have no choice but to drop him.

United made it back to Wembley for the 2017 EFL Cup Final in February, but Marcus spent most of the match on the bench. And when he did come on, he struck his one good chance straight at the Southampton keeper. Noooo! It was the same old story, with Zlatan saving the day for United instead.

Marcus was pleased to pick up another winner's medal, but he didn't feel like he fully deserved it. He had lost his magic touch! Oh well, he just had to stay strong and keep believing; that's what he'd learnt from Ibra. This was just another obstacle that he had to overcome.

Away at Sunderland, Marcus came on for Jesse with half an hour to go. United were already 2–0 up against the team in twentieth place. Surely, he wouldn't get a better chance to end his goal drought.

But before he knew it, they were into the last five minutes and Marcus still hadn't even had a shot. 'Nooooooooo!' Was he going to go yet another league game without a goal?

In the very last minute, he raced down the right wing and then passed inside to Zlatan. He thought about shooting himself, but instead, he slipped it back to Marcus, who was now into the penalty area. This was it – his big moment to score.

'Go back to basics' – that's what everyone had told him to do: Zlatan, Mourinho, Wayne, Giggsy. 'Just pick a spot and shoot.' Marcus kept his cool, even as the Sunderland defender slid in to try and tackle him. *BANG!* His shot flew past Jordan Pickford and into the bottom corner.

Goooooooooooooooooooaaaaaaaaaaaaaaaallllllllllll llllllllllllllll!!!!!!!!!!!!!!!!!!!

As he got up off the grass, Marcus threw his arms high into the air. Yes, another Premier League goal at last!

'Thanks for passing!' he shouted to Zlatan as they shared a high-five.

'No problem, you needed that. Now you've just got to keep on scoring!'

Zlatan's wise words became even more important a few weeks later, when he injured his knee in the Europa League. Could Marcus step up and be United's match-winner instead?

CHAPTER 17

EUROPEAN GLORY

'Arghhhh!' Zlatan cried out as he collapsed onto the grass in agony.

It was 1–1 in the ninetieth minute of United's Europa League quarter-final second leg against the Belgian club, Anderlecht, and their star striker had just picked up a horrible injury.

After jumping up to win the ball, Zlatan had landed awkwardly, twisting his right knee. Everyone knew that he wasn't the kind of guy who went down easily. Uh oh, what were United going to do without him?

Marcus was already on the pitch, playing on the left wing, but Mourinho decided to move him into the middle. This was his chance to show that he was a top striker who could take over from Zlatan.

'Come on!' the United fans urged him on.

Despite his struggles in the Premier League, Marcus was enjoying a good spell in the Europa League. After all, that was where his United career had started, with those two goals against FC Midtjylland. He loved the competition.

Under Mourinho, Marcus wasn't scoring so often, but he was getting better and better at setting up goals for others:

One for Zlatan against Saint-Étienne,

One for Henrikh in the first leg against Anderlecht,

And another for Henrikh earlier on in the second leg.

He was creating lots of chances for his teammates, but now Marcus needed to be United's main striker. His job in extra-time was to shoot his team into the Europa League semi-finals.

'I can do this,' he told himself, as calm and focused as ever. He knew that he would have to do a lot better than his earlier efforts in the game:

A long-range strike that he dragged well wide,

A left-foot shot that hit the side netting,

And a one-on-one where he took the ball around the keeper, but his touch was too heavy.

'Noooooooo!' Marcus screamed out in frustration. What was going on? He was normally so good at one-on-ones.

Marcus had to find his shooting boots again, and quickly. Otherwise, United would be out.

Early in the second half of extra-time, Marouane headed the ball down to Marcus just inside the crowded Anderlecht penalty area. What an opportunity! His first touch was beautiful to bring it under control, and his second was even better.

Just as a defender dived in for the block, Marcus dragged the ball back. Cruyff Turn! He was on his weaker left foot now and a little off-balance too, but he still knew exactly where the bottom corner was.

Goooooooooooooooooooaaaaaaaaaaaaaaallllllllllll llllllllllllllll!!!!!!!!!!!!!!!!!!!!

It wasn't one of Marcus's best strikes, but it was certainly one of his most important goals. When his team needed him most, he had delivered. United were only thirteen minutes away from the semi-finals now. Looking up at the fans, he leapt high into the air, his fists clenched with passion.

'Come onnnnnnn!' he roared.

Sadly, Zlatan's season was over, which meant that Marcus was now Manchester United's first-choice striker. So, could he lead his club to the Europa League final? Yes!

'Keep a clean sheet and try to get an away goal.' That was Mourinho's plan for the first leg against Celta Vigo. The defence stayed strong, and Marcus did the rest. In the twentieth minute, he curled a powerful shot towards the top corner, but the keeper tipped it past the post. So close!

There was nothing that the keeper could do to stop Marcus's fantastic free kick in the second half, however. From wide on the right, it looked like Daley Blind would cross it in with his left foot, but instead, he dummied it for Marcus. United's striker had won the free kick in the first place, and now he was going to take it himself. With a whip of his right foot, he sent the ball swerving into the far corner of the net. 1–0!

*Gooooooooooooooooooooaaaaaaaaaaaaaaaaaalllllllllllll
llllllllllllllll!!!!!!!!!!!!!!!!!!!!!!!*

Job done! And back at Old Trafford, Marcus made
sure of the victory with another moment of magic.
From the left wing, he swung in a perfect cross for
Marouane to head home at the back post. It was 2–0
– and United were into the Europa League Final!

'And we're going to win it!' Marcus and Paul
celebrated together.

Their opponents in Athens would be Ajax, one
of the best young teams in the world. They had
Davinson Sánchez and Matthijs de Ligt at the back,
Hakim Ziyech and Davy Klaassen in midfield, and
Kasper Dolberg in attack.

United certainly had a lot more experience in their
line-up, plus one of the most exciting young strikers
on the planet.

Marcus wasn't fazed by a big European final. He
had already won twice at Wembley and also played for
England at the Euros. So as the two teams walked out
onto the pitch, he looked as calmly confident as ever.

United were going to win, and they were determined to win it for Manchester. Just two days earlier, twenty-two people had tragically died following a terrorist attack at an Ariana Grande concert in the city. The local people were still shocked and distraught, but Marcus and his teammates would do their best to bring them back a bit of joy, and a trophy too.

In the sixteenth minute of the game, Marcus played a neat one-two with Juan on the edge of the Ajax box. Patiently, they worked the ball across to Marouane and finally to Paul. *BANG!* His shot took a big deflection off Sánchez, giving the keeper no chance of stopping it. *1–0!*

'Yessss!' Marcus cried out, racing over to celebrate with Paul.

Early in the second half, Henrikh scored a second goal, and Ajax couldn't come back from that. United were the new Europa League Champions! And to make things even better, they would now be playing in the Champions League next season.

'Hurraaaaaaaay!' Marcus hadn't been the hero this time, but he had worked really hard for his team, up front on his own; making runs, battling for the ball, and causing lots of problems for the Ajax centre-backs. This time, in the final, he had definitely played his part.

At the final whistle, Marcus had hugs for everyone: Henrikh, Juan, Jesse, Paul, Daley, Michael, Marouane, his old academy mate Axel... And Zlatan, who had come all the way to Greece to cheer his teammates on to European glory.

'Great game, great win!' he congratulated Marcus.

Later that night, United's two top strikers posed for a photo together with the trophy. On one side, a football legend; on the other, a future superstar.

CHAPTER 18

NEW SEASON, SAME POSITION

With Zlatan out injured for at least another six months, would Marcus be Manchester United's main striker for the start of the 2017–18 season? He looked taller, stronger and better than ever when he returned for pre-season training. He now felt ready for the extra responsibility.

But despite Marcus's key role in their Europa League glory, Mourinho had a different plan. In order to compete for the Premier League title, he wanted a big, reliable, goalscoring Number 9, not an inconsistent but talented teenager who was still growing. So United signed Romelu Lukaku from Everton for £75 million.

For Marcus, that meant new season, same position
– left wing. Oh well – it didn't matter where he
played, just as long as he played. And played well.

Marcus dribbled forward at full speed from deep in
his own half, bursting into the space behind the West
Ham right-back. In a flash, he was almost on the
edge of the penalty area...

'Yes!' Romelu called for it, pointing towards the
gap between the centre-backs. Marcus knew exactly
what kind of pass a striker would want. He delivered
the perfect through-ball for United's new Number 9
to strike first time. *1–0!*

As he raced away to celebrate, Romelu pointed
again, this time at Marcus. 'What a ball!' he cried
out, thanking him with a bear hug.

Marcus was happy to help his teammates, but he
preferred getting the goals himself. Nothing could
beat that buzz. He scored:

One against Leicester City,

One against Stoke City,

One against Basel on his Champions League debut,

And two against Burton Albion in the EFL Cup.

Five goals in five games! It was so far so good for the new season.

With United competing for four trophies, Marcus couldn't play every minute of every match. But whether he started the game, or came on as a super sub, he always did his best to make an impact. He celebrated his twentieth birthday by coming off the bench in the Champions League against Benfica.

'Over here, Rom – pass it!'

After only one minute on the pitch, Marcus was already on the attack, sprinting past the right-back and into the Benfica box. He twisted and turned his way past one defender, then tried to squeeze his way in between two more, until eventually they fouled him. Penalty!

'Nice run, Rash!' Romelu said, helping him back up to his feet.

Marcus was now up to seven goals and five assists for the season, and November hadn't even started yet!

By January, however, his great form had faded, and he found himself back on the bench again. Even when Mourinho gave Romelu a rest, it was Anthony who played up front instead.

And on the left wing? Well, United had just signed Alexis Sánchez from Arsenal. So at most, Marcus was getting fifteen minutes at the end of matches to try to create some magic.

'Now I'm never going to get my form back!' he told his brothers miserably. He needed the rhythm of regular game-time to get his season back on track.

'Hey, just keep working hard,' they tried to reassure him. 'And be patient – remember, you're only twenty!'

Marcus nodded. It was easy to forget sometimes just how young he still was. But by February, he was hardly playing for United. Sometimes, he wasn't even in Mourinho's matchday squad at all.

'Where's Rashford?' the fans wondered when they looked at the team sheet against Newcastle. 'Is he injured?'

It was a tough time for Marcus, but he didn't give up. He was too determined for that. All he needed was one more opportunity...

Away at Crystal Palace in early March, United

were 1–0 down at half-time. What was Mourinho going to do now? Romelu, Jesse and Alexis were already on the pitch, and Anthony was out injured… So the manager took off a midfielder and brought on Marcus.

Wow, a whole forty-five minutes! But things actually got worse before they got better. Early in the second half, Palace scored again from a quick free kick. *2–0!*

Uh oh. United really needed a gamechanger now. Although Marcus didn't get a goal or an assist, he helped to turn things around. With his positive forward runs, he pushed his team further and further up the pitch, in search of goals.

Chris Smalling headed in the first, then Romelu equalised, then Nemanja scored a screamer. What an incredible comeback: 3–2 to United!

After that, Mourinho simply *had* to start Marcus in the next league match: at home against Liverpool. It was one of the biggest rivalries in British football, and a game that United always had to win. But how? Playing on the left wing, Marcus would be up against

Trent Alexander-Arnold, a young right-back who was known for his attacking, rather than his defending.

'Use your speed to get in behind him,' Mourinho told Marcus. 'Go out there and give him the hardest game of his young career!'

'Yes, Boss!'

In the fourteenth minute, David sent a long goal-kick upfield towards Romelu. As he jumped for the ball with Dejan Lovren, Marcus was already on the move behind him, hoping for the flick-on. By the time that Alexander-Arnold saw the danger, it was already too late for Liverpool.

ZOOM! Marcus burst into the box, Cruyff-turned his way onto his right foot and,

BANG! He fired a shot into the far corner. *1–0!*

Gooooooooooooooooooooaaaaaaaaaaaaaaaalllllllllllll llllllllllllll!!!!!!!!!!!!!!!!!!!!

As Old Trafford went wild all around him, Marcus raced over to celebrate with the fans. He was one of them, after all.

'Yes Rash, what a strike!' Ashley Young yelled, wrapping him in a tight hug.

Ten minutes later, Marcus did it again. This time, as Romelu and Alexis attacked through the middle, he stayed out wide on the left. Virgil van Dijk eventually tackled Alexis, but the ball bounced out to the edge of the area…

Alexander-Arnold had chased back to help the other defenders, leaving Marcus all alone with the ball travelling towards him. He didn't think; he just hit it, low into the far corner again. *2–0!*

Goooooooooooooooooooooaaaaaaaaaaaaaaaaaalllllllllllll lllllllllllllll!!!!!!!!!!!!!!!!!!!!!!

With his arms outstretched, Marcus stood by the corner flag and soaked up all the cheers and applause. What a feeling! Scoring two goals against Liverpool was enough to make you a Manchester United hero for life.

The overall season would go down as a disappointing one for Marcus, but with performances like that one, his time would definitely come soon.

CHAPTER 19

2018 WORLD CUP

Gareth Southgate announced his England squad for the 2018 World Cup with a special video, where each player's name was revealed one by one. Raheem Sterling was first, then John Stones, then Trent Alexander-Arnold…

Eventually, two kids appeared on screen, standing in a Manchester street. One was wearing a red England shirt and he turned around to show the name on the back:

'Marcus… RASHFORD!' they cheered together. 'The boy wonder.'

His Euro 2016 call-up had been a total shock, but Marcus wasn't surprised to be in the 2018

World Cup squad. He had been playing well for his country for a while now. Even so, it was an amazing moment, and another childhood dream come true.

'After years of you standing on the touch line in the cold and rain, Mum we're off to the World Cup!' he tweeted with a picture of Melanie looking proud.

Marcus had been busy training with United on the morning of the big announcement, but he returned home to find lots of nice messages from his friends and family. He tried to play it cool like usual, but inside he was buzzing with excitement.

'Russia, here we come!' he messaged Jesse.

Would they return home as World Cup heroes? Ahead of the tournament, Southgate had switched the formation from a 4–3–3 to a 3–5–2 with wing-backs. It meant one more player in midfield, and one less player in attack.

That was good news for Jesse, and bad news for Marcus. Harry and Raheem were England's first-choice forwards, but hopefully he could come on and be the super sub. If the team needed someone to make an impact off the bench, then he would be ready and waiting.

Marcus sent out a final 'Pick me!' to Southgate in the team's last friendly against Costa Rica. In the thirteenth minute, he got the ball on the right, with time and space to think. What next? In a flash, he spotted that the keeper had come forward a little, off his goal line.

Some players might have seen it and thought, 'No, not worth trying', but Marcus was confident enough to give anything a go. *BANG!* Before the poor keeper knew what was going on, the ball was dipping and swerving over his head… and into the far corner of the net. *1–0!*

Goooooooooooooooooooooaaaaaaaaaaaaaaaalllllllllllll llllllllllllll!!!!!!!!!!!!!!!!!!!!

It was one of his best strikes ever, but Marcus didn't show any emotion. He just threw his arms out and walked away, as if he did that every day. Yes, if England needed a moment of World Cup magic, he would be ready and waiting.

In the first match in Volgograd, against Tunisia, it didn't look like they'd need Marcus at all. Harry scored an early goal and England were cruising, but out of nowhere, Tunisia scored a penalty. Suddenly it was 1–1, and a draw wouldn't do for England.

In the sixty-eighth minute, Marcus came on for Raheem. On his World Cup debut, what could he do to help his country?

'Our passing's too slow,' he signalled to his teammates. 'We've got to move it around more quickly!'

Marcus ran and ran, desperate to do something special. It was only in the final five minutes, however, that he was able to get himself on the ball and into the game. With a burst of speed, he dribbled down the right wing and won another corner for England.

Come on!

Seconds later, as Ruben Loftus-Cheek cut the ball back, Marcus was in space near the penalty spot. Perfect! This was it: his chance to score the winner. But then…

'Leave it!' he heard Jesse shout at the last second.

But when Marcus dummied it, the ball got stuck under Jesse's feet.

'Nooooooo!' Marcus snarled, turning away in anger.

Thankfully, Harry scored a last-minute header to give England the victory. Phew!

'In our first game, it's just good to get the three points,' Marcus told the media afterwards, sounding so mature for his age. 'Now we can relax our way into the tournament.'

In their second group match, even without Marcus on the pitch, England thrashed Panama 6–1. Although he was sad to miss out on such a goal-fest, he did get to start the next match against Marouane's Belgium.

Both nations were already through to the Round of 16, and so the managers rested their stars. But for squad players like Marcus, it was a massive opportunity. Raheem had now gone twenty-two games without a goal for England. Many fans were already calling for Marcus to play instead, so if he could score against Belgium...

Sadly, Marcus failed to take the few chances he got. He curled his first shot way past the post and then missed a crucial one-on-one against Thibaut Courtois.

'Come on, you've got to do better than that!' he shouted at himself.

England lost 1–0, Belgium won the group, and Marcus moved back to the bench. His World Cup, however, wasn't over yet.

In the Round of 16 against Colombia, Southgate brought Marcus on as England's fourth substitute, deep in extra-time. There was one obvious reason for that: PENALTIES! Yes, it looked like they were heading for another horrible shoot-out, and for that, England would need their coolest, calmest players on the pitch.

Nothing fazed Marcus; he was totally fearless. But as he walked forward to take England's second spot-kick, all three penalties so far had been scored. The pressure was on.

'Go on, Rash!' Jordan shouted as he threw the ball to him.

With quick, confident strides, Marcus entered the penalty area and placed it down carefully on the spot. As he stepped back to start his run-up, he fixed his eyes first on the ball and then on the goal in front of him. That helped him to focus and ignore the noise of the crowd.

After four little shuffles to the left, Marcus moved forward, taking short steps to try to fool the keeper. David Ospina did guess the right way, but Marcus tucked the ball right into the bottom corner. *GOAL!*

Ice-cold! He didn't celebrate at all; not even a fist pump. Instead, Marcus jogged over to Jordan to give him some encouragement. It worked. Six spot-kicks later, England had won the shoot-out. They were into the World Cup quarter-finals!

'Yessssssssss!' Marcus didn't join the big player pile-up, but he stood next to it, smiling. What a moment, what an achievement! He was so proud to be a part of English football history.

And their Russian adventure continued. The quarter-final finished England 2 Sweden 0. Easy! Marcus had only come on for the last minute, but winning was one big squad effort. Everyone could see that, especially the fans back home. They had fallen in love with the national team again.

There were high hopes for the semi-final against

Croatia and it started so well. In the fifth minute, Kieran Trippier curled a free kick into the top corner. 1–0!

'Get in!' Marcus punched the air on the sidelines.

But in the second half, as England tired, Croatia seemed to grow stronger. With twenty minutes to go, Ivan Perišić got the equaliser. *1–1!*

'Marcus, get ready – you're coming on!'

'Yes, Coach!'

With his fast, fresh legs, Marcus was determined to make an impact. He chased after every long punt and pass, putting the Croatian defenders under pressure. If only he could get one good chance...

As the ball dropped, Domagoj Vida missed his header and for a second, it looked like Marcus might be in. But it bounced up over his head and the Croatian keeper rushed out to collect it.

'Ohhhhhhhhh!' groaned every England player and supporter, including Marcus.

He kept chasing everything right until the end of extra-time, but by then, Croatia had scored the winning goal. It was all over, and England were out of the World Cup.

At the final whistle, Marcus collapsed onto the grass, his hands covering the tears streaming down his face. It was a devastating feeling, one of the worst he had ever experienced. He had given absolutely everything, and yet it hadn't been enough.

'Hey, you've been brilliant,' Southgate said, helping him back up. 'You should be so proud of what you've achieved!'

Although his manager was right, it didn't feel that way out there on the pitch in Moscow. It was so disappointing to come so close. As the players stood in front of the fans, thanking them for all their support, Marcus was already thinking ahead to next time.

Next time, he would be starring in the starting line-up.

And next time, he would lead England all the way to the World Cup final.

CHAPTER 20

UNITED'S NEW NUMBER 10

Marcus returned from the 2018 World Cup feeling more determined than ever. He was going to make this his greatest year yet at Old Trafford, the season where he went from inconsistent kid to reliable scorer, from 'Boy Wonder' to 'Star Striker'. It was time. Marcus was nearly twenty-one now, and he was also United's new Number 10.

Wow, what an honour! That shirt had been worn by so many of the club's most famous forwards:

Denis Law,

Mark Hughes,

Teddy Sheringham,

Ruud van Nistelrooy,

And, of course, Wayne Rooney, his hero and mentor.

'It suits you mate,' he wrote on social media when Marcus first wore his old number.

It was one of his proudest moments, especially as a lifelong Manchester United fan. Now, Marcus had to prove himself worthy to wear the shirt. He had scored seven Premier League goals last season and now he was looking to double that, at least.

'Let's do this!' he said with one arm around Romelu and the other around Anthony. They were Numbers 9, 10 and 11 now and between them, they had everything they needed to become one of the best attacking trios in Europe.

The new season didn't start the way Marcus had hoped, however. After a win against Leicester, they lost to Brighton and then, things would get even worse against Burnley, despite a promising start: United were already winning 2–0 when he came on. It should have been a nice, comfortable afternoon, but instead, he surprisingly lost his cool.

As Marcus tried to dribble past Phil Bardsley, the

Burnley right-back kicked the ball out for a corner and then took a second, angry kick at him.

'Hey!' Marcus cried out as he fell to the floor. 'You can't do that!'

When he got back up, Marcus walked over towards Bardsley. He was so furious that he made the mistake of going head-to-head with the defender.

'Ref!' Bardsley called out, touching his head and pretending to be in pain. 'Did you see that?'

The referee ran over and reached into his pocket: RED CARD!

What? Marcus couldn't believe it. At first, he blamed Bardsley and the referee, but once he had calmed down a bit in the dressing room, he realised it was really his own fault. How could he be so stupid? He had fallen for the oldest trick in the book!

'Sorry to everyone at the club and all the fans,' Marcus wrote on Twitter. He had learnt his lesson.

After that bad start to a fresh chapter as United's new Number 10, Marcus soon bounced back. He wasn't yet banging in the goals every game, but he showed flashes of his brilliance. He scored a flick volley against West Ham, he caught the Fulham keeper out at his near post, and he grabbed a last-minute winner away at Bournemouth.

'Come on!' Marcus roared as he raced over to the United fans in the corner. That was more like it; he was scoring goals when his team needed him most.

Although it was an important win, there was still plenty of room for improvement. United were meant to be challenging for the Premier League title, or at least the Top Four, but instead, they were way down in eighth place. That simply wasn't good enough, especially with such a talented and expensive squad.

'We spent £90 million on Pogba – what a waste of money that was!' some supporters moaned. 'And what's happened to Rashford? I thought he was going to be as good as Mbappé!'

All was not well at Old Trafford. In December, the club directors decided that it was time for another fresh start. They were going to replace Mourinho with a new manager, and announced that, until the end of the season, that would be Ole Gunnar Solskjær, the legendary striker who had scored United's winning goal in the 1999 Champions League final.

The atmosphere at the club seemed to change straight away. Suddenly, everyone was excited again:

Ole's at the wheel,
Tell me how does it feel,
We've got Sanchez, Paul Pogba and Fred,
Marcus Rashford, a Manc born and bred,
Duh du, du du du du du
Duh du, du du du du du!

Solskjær was certainly a fans' favourite, but could he really help to turn things around at Old Trafford? As a fellow striker, Marcus had a good feeling about it.

CHAPTER 21

SCORING AGAIN UNDER SOLSKJÆR

Solskjær's first message to the Manchester United players was clear and simple: 'I want us to play forward and I was us to play fast.'

After all, what was the point in having the power of Paul and the pace of Marcus and Anthony in attack if they weren't going to use it properly? The plan was to bring back the style of the United of old, the one that had won so many trophies under Sir Alex Ferguson. That team had been impossible to stop, and also exciting to watch.

'Yeah!' everyone agreed eagerly.

There was lots of work to be done first, however, all over the pitch. As a former striker himself,

Solskjær focused on helping the forwards in particular. He could understand Marcus's amazing potential – his speed, his skill, his strength, his intelligence – but he could also see the weaknesses in his game.

'I want you to be our star striker from now on,' the manager encouraged him. 'I know you can do it, but you need to score more goals. So let's turn you into a clinical finisher!'

Together, they worked hard on Marcus's movement in the box and, most importantly, his composure in front of goal.

'Don't rush the shot!' Solskjær kept telling him. 'Take your time, stay calm and pick your spot. The goal's not going to move!'

Soon, Marcus was ready to put that finishing into practice on the pitch. Meanwhile, Solskjær continued to assemble his squad for his first match as United manager. He picked:

Anthony on the left,

Jesse on the right,

And Marcus in the middle!

Marcus knew his new manager really believed in him, and that gave him a much-needed boost. Now, it was time to say thanks.

In the second minute of the away match against Cardiff City, the opposition gave away a free kick just outside their penalty area. And up stepped Marcus to blast the ball into the bottom corner. *1–0!*

Goooooooooooooooooooooaaaaaaaaaaaaaaaallllllllllll lllllllllllllll!!!!!!!!!!!!!!!!!!!!!!!

At the full-time whistle, United were 5–1 winners. What a start!

Marcus was delighted to score another fantastic free kick, but he kept thinking about the one-on-one that he had missed in the second half. Despite staying calm and picking his spot, the Cardiff keeper had deflected his shot wide. Had Marcus rushed his finish again? Should he have aimed for the other side instead?

'Hey, don't worry about it,' Solskjær reassured him. 'You'll score that next time.'

Marcus was a man on a mission. In the fourth minute against Bournemouth, he danced his way through their defence with Ronaldo-esque footwork.

He poked the ball past the first, then did an elástico to escape from the second, before crossing it for Paul to tap in. 1–0!

Marcus had an assist; now he wanted a goal of his own. At the end of the first half, Anthony delivered a deep cross towards the Bournemouth back post. With a burst of speed, Marcus got to it first, stretched out his right boot, and somehow flicked the ball into the opposite corner of the net. *3–0!*

Goooooooooooooooooooooaaaaaaaaaaaaaaaaallllllllllll llllllllllllllll!!!!!!!!!!!!!!!!!!!!

With Solskjær's support, Marcus was back to his absolute best, and it was beautiful to watch. He was playing almost every minute of every United match.

Away at Newcastle, Alexis passed it through to Marcus, who was unmarked on the edge of the six-yard box. It was one of those chances that a star striker simply had to score. As the keeper rushed out towards him, Marcus took one touch to control the ball and then calmly placed it past Martin Dúbravka. *2–0!*

Goooooooooooooooooooooaaaaaaaaaaaaaaaaallllllllllll llllllllllllllll!!!!!!!!!!!!!!!!!!!!

On the sidelines, Solskjær clapped and smiled. Much better, Marcus!

'He's got frightening pace, he's now become stronger, he can hold the ball up for us and he's a great link player,' the United manager told the media. 'He can become a top, top player.'

Now that Marcus had finally found his striker's rhythm, the goals were flooding in.

Away at Tottenham, Paul spotted Marcus's run and played the perfect long pass. As he reached the ball on the edge of the penalty area, Marcus thought about hitting it first time, but then he heard his manager's voice in his head:

'Don't rush the shot!'

So instead, he took a touch and carefully picked his spot. *BANG!* – bottom corner. *1–0!*

Goooooooooooooooooooooaaaaaaaaaaaaaaaaallllllllllllll llllllllllllllll!!!!!!!!!!!!!!!!!!!

It was a brilliant strike from a very difficult angle, but Marcus made it look so easy. His finishing was improving with every game and every goal.

'Come on!' he shouted, punching the air with

passion. He was getting used to that great goalscoring feeling. He scored the winners for United against Brighton and Leicester City too.

Six goals in eight games! That took him up to nine for the Premier League season, his best-ever total. At last, this was the big breakthrough that Marcus had been working towards; his move from 'Boy Wonder' to 'Star Striker'.

One of his old teammates agreed: 'Rashford is the future of Manchester United,' Zlatan announced. 'Now he is using his quality more for the team, not just for himself. He has big potential – he has no limits.'

In the Champions League, Marcus came face-to-face with Europe's top wonderkid, Kylian Mbappé. Let the battle begin! The Frenchman won the first leg, scoring PSG's second goal at Old Trafford, but it was Marcus who won the second leg in Paris.

First, he hit a long-range rocket that Gianluigi Buffon couldn't hold. Romelu raced in to grab the rebound. *GOAL!*

'Come on, we can do this!' Marcus cheered with confidence.

Then, in the very last minute, just when it looked like it was all over for United, they won a penalty. And after four long minutes of VAR and arguing, it was Marcus who stepped up to take it. It was the biggest moment of his football career, but he was a calm, clinical, world-class finisher now.

Goooooooooooooooooooaaaaaaaaaaaaaaaaaallllllllllll llllllllllllll!!!!!!!!!!!!!!!!!!!

'Yes, Rash!'

'What a hero!' his teammates cheered as they chased him over to the corner flag.

United were through to the Champions League quarter-finals, thanks to their new star striker.

Unfortunately, their form soon fizzled out after that, but for Marcus, the most important thing was making progress. As a team, they were starting to play more exciting football, and as a striker, he was starting to look like a more lethal finisher. 2018–19 had been his best scoring season so far, and 2019–20 was going to be even better.

CHAPTER 22

FINDING THE NET IN THE NATIONS LEAGUE

Marcus was starting to get more game-time for England too. After the 2018 World Cup, Southgate decided to switch formation again, this time back to a 4–3–3. Suddenly, there was space for three forwards in the team: Raheem, Harry and one more… Marcus!

Although he was the most popular choice, there was plenty of competition: Danny Welbeck, James Maddison, Callum Wilson, and Jadon Sancho, the new boy wonder on the block. Jadon was only eighteen and he was already playing brilliantly on the right wing for Borussia Dortmund in Germany.

'Man, you're making me feel old!' Marcus joked.

He knew that he would need to work hard to secure that starting spot, starting with the UEFA Nations League. It was a brand-new European tournament and England were up against two of the top teams in the world: Spain and their World Cup rivals, Croatia. Wow, it wouldn't be easy, but Marcus always loved a challenge.

'They're going to be really good games for us,' he said in an interview. 'We have to start beating these bigger countries in the world and there's no two better opponents to do that against.'

In order to win, England would need goals, and not just from Harry. So far, Marcus had only scored three international goals in twenty-five appearances. Okay, so he had come off the bench in a lot of those games, but still, it was a disappointing record for someone who was supposed to be a striker. It was time to change that.

At Wembley, England got off to the perfect start against Spain. As Harry spread the ball out to Luke Shaw on the left, Marcus was already in position, between the defenders, and ready to make his move.

'Now!' he called out, bursting into the box.

Luke's pass was perfect and so was Marcus's finish, past their United teammate, David. *1–0!*

Gooooooooooooooooooooaaaaaaaaaaaaaaaaalllllllllllll llllllllllllll!!!!!!!!!!!!!!!!!!!!!!

Marcus didn't race away to celebrate; he jogged. He was Mr Cool, especially in front of goal these days. For United, and now for England too.

Sadly, Spain fought back to win 2–1, but Marcus knew that the team was moving in the right direction. He certainly was. Three days later, in a friendly against Switzerland, he snuck in at the back post to volley home the winner.

'What a finish, Rash!' Danny Rose shouted, giving him a big hug.

Two in two – England had a new star striker now!

Marcus missed a couple of good chances in the disappointing 0–0 draw against Croatia, but he didn't let that get him down. Instead, he looked forward, to England's second game against Spain. It was now a must-win match. Otherwise, they had no chance of making it to the Nations League Finals.

'Come on, we can do this!' Southgate told his team before kick-off.

For Marcus, it felt like a massive moment in his international career. If he failed, Jadon was there, waiting impatiently on the bench, ready to take his place. But if he succeeded...

For the first forty magnificent minutes, England's exciting new front three destroyed the Spanish defence together.

First, Harry passed to Marcus, who delivered a dangerous cross to Raheem. *1–0!*

Then Harry slipped a brilliant pass through to Marcus, who calmly fired a shot into the bottom corner. *2–0!*

And finally, Harry slid the ball across to Raheem in the six-yard box. *3–0!*

'Yesssss!' Marcus punched the air with pride. The England attack was on fire, and they were having so much fun together. Their speed, their skill, their movement and their shooting; they were too hot for even top defenders like Sergio Ramos to handle.

Although Spain fought back in the second half

once again, this time, England held on for a huge
3–2 victory.

'Top work tonight!' Southgate told Marcus with a
smile and hug as the squad celebrated out on the pitch.

'Thanks, Boss!'

Hopefully, with more goals and more performances
like that, Marcus could secure his place alongside
Raheem and Harry in attack.

'Rashford is a tremendous talent,' Southgate
confirmed, just in case anyone still doubted it.

With a 2–1 win over Croatia, England made it
through to the Nations League Finals, where they
faced the Netherlands in the semis. Harry was out
injured, so Marcus was now England's central striker,
up against two of the best defenders in the world:
Virgil van Dijk and Matthijs de Ligt.

'Bring it on!' Marcus had given de Ligt a tough
game in the Europa League final back in 2017; now,
it was time to test him again.

In the thirtieth minute, the Netherlands were
looking very comfortable as they passed the ball
around at the back. But as it came to de Ligt, he lost

his concentration and let it slip under his foot. It
was only a half-mistake, but that was all that Marcus
needed. In a sprint race, he could beat almost
anyone. He got to the ball first, just before de Ligt,
who kicked Marcus's shin instead. *Penalty!*

He picked himself up and put the ball down on the
spot. Without Harry, Marcus was England's penalty
taker now. No problem! After four little shuffles to
the left, he moved forward, taking short steps to try
to fool the keeper. It worked. As Jasper Cillessen
dived to his right, Marcus placed his shot in the
opposite corner. *1–0!*

*Goooooooooooooooooooaaaaaaaaaaaaaaaaalllllllllllll
lllllllllllll!!!!!!!!!!!!!!!!!!!!*

As cool as you like! He jogged over to the England
fans, holding up the Three Lions on his shirt. Harry
who? Marcus was a top finisher too!

When the second half started, however, he wasn't
out there on the pitch. Marcus had tried his best to
ignore his injured ankle, but eventually, it was just
too painful to play on.

'Good luck, lads!' he told his teammates.

Without Marcus, however, England lost their way. From 1–0 up, they fell to a 3–1 defeat and crashed out of the competition.

It was a disappointing way to end, but overall, Marcus had enjoyed his first Nations League experience. Hopefully his three goals had earned him a regular England starting spot, especially with the next Euros coming up soon.

CHAPTER 23

UNITED'S STAR STRIKER

30 October 2019, Stamford Bridge, London

Almost three months into the new season, and Manchester United were still struggling to find their form. Their new star striker, however, had certainly found his. Marcus's scoring run had started on the opening day with two classy finishes against Chelsea. Now, United were on their way to Stamford Bridge to take on Chelsea again, this time in the Carabao Cup fourth round.

As the team travelled down to London, Marcus had every reason to feel confident. It had been a fantastic week for him. First, he had converted

Daniel James' cross to end Liverpool's seventeen-match winning streak, and then he had calmly slotted home against Norwich City. That was his fifth goal of the season and his fiftieth for United.

Two in two! Even a missed penalty wasn't going to get him down. Harry Kane, Sergio Agüero, Pierre-Emerick Aubameyang, and Marcus Rashford – *that's* where he was aiming to be, amongst the most prolific strikers in the Premier League.

'Yes!' Marcus called out for the ball, as Daniel dribbled up the right wing. He was in space on the edge of the area, in between two Chelsea defenders. Daniel, however, decided to go it alone. He danced his way into the box, where Marcos Alonso brought him down. *Penalty to United!*

'Great work!' Marcus told Daniel, quickly grabbing the ball. He was determined to take it, despite that miss against Norwich.

Marcus went through his usual spot-kick routine, but faster this time, as if he couldn't wait to… SCORE! *1–0!*

Gooooooooooooaaaaaaaaaaalllllllllllllllllll!!!!!!!!!!!!!!!

It was a perfect penalty, sending the keeper the wrong way. As Marcus and his teammates celebrated with cool high-fives, their manager, Solskjær, punched the air with both fists. Thank goodness their star striker was on fire!

United's lead lasted all the way until the sixtieth minute, when Michy Batshuayi scored a superb solo goal. 1–1! Uh oh, the pressure was back on the team in red. They needed something special from their star striker, otherwise their cup run would be over.

In the seventy-second minute, Fred won a free kick for United, thirty-five yards out from the Chelsea goal. It would take a wonderstrike to beat Willy Caballero from there, but Marcus was always up for a challenge.

Although he was getting better and better at scoring tap-ins these days, he still preferred the spectacular long-range rockets he hit like those of Cristiano Ronaldo. Those were the shots that Marcus practised most after training, and they were the goals that he remembered most too. That free kick against Celta Vigo in the Europa League semi-final, that dipping, swerving shot for England versus Costa Rica; those were moments that Marcus would never ever forget.

It was time to add one more to that incredible collection, on the night before his twenty-second birthday. One, two, three steps and then BANG! As soon as the ball left his boot, Marcus knew that it was a good, clean strike. He watched it fly high over the jumping heads in the Chelsea wall...

'Now, down and a little to the left!' Marcus muttered, as if the ball could hear him.

Maybe it could because not only did it dip, but it also swerved, away from Caballero and into the top corner. 2–1!

Goooooooooooooooooooaaaaaaaaaaaaaaaaaalllllllllllllllll llllllllllll!!!!!!!!!!!!!!!!!!!!

It was a beauty, easily one of the best he had ever scored. What a way to win a match! Marcus raced away to celebrate, sliding on his knees towards the United fans in the corner.

'You hero!' Ashley screamed, hugging him tightly as he got back up to his feet.

'Come on!' Marcus roared over his teammate's shoulder.

There was nothing he loved more than scoring spectacular strikes for his club. Like his hero Cristiano, he was now combining skills with goals. Marcus was so proud to be United's new Number 10, their consistent star striker at last.

After that stunner at Stamford Bridge, the goals kept coming. Now that he had found his rhythm, suddenly Marcus just couldn't stop scoring: against Partizan Belgrade in the Europe League; then back in the Premier League against Brighton, Sheffield United, two against Tottenham, and then one in United's Manchester derby win over City.

Marcus didn't even have to think about it anymore; he just shot and scored. Simple!

He grabbed one against Colchester in the Carabao Cup quarter-finals, then one against Newcastle, one against Burnley, and another two against Norwich.

Wow, it was still only January, and Marcus was already up to nineteen goals for the season! He had well and truly smashed all of his previous scoring records.

'Rashford is really starting to look like the real deal,' one journalist wrote. 'He now deserves to be called world class.'

Nearly four years after his dream debut against FC Midtjylland, Marcus was at last living up to those early expectations. There had been tough times along the way, but he had never stopped believing in himself and his ability. Now, it was official; the boy wonder had become United's star striker.

And a few months later, Marcus made another massive leap, this time from football hero to national hero. Despite all the fame and fortune of playing for Manchester United and England, he had never forgotten his younger years in Wythenshawe. Back then, his mum, Melanie, had worked so hard to put food on the table for the family. And if it weren't for the free meals that he got at school, some days Marcus might have gone hungry.

So when the schools closed during the devastating coronavirus pandemic and those free meals stopped, he knew that he had to do something to help. Once upon a time, he had been one of the children who relied on that food and without it, Marcus might not have gone on to achieve his football dreams. He couldn't just sit back and let those kids go hungry; this was his chance to make a difference, to be a gamechanger off the football pitch, as well as on it.

Teaming up with a charity called FareShare, Marcus helped raise almost £1 million. Wow, that was enough money to provide more than 3 million meals per week to vulnerable children across the country!

'Thank you all SO much for the support,' he tweeted. 'And whilst I'm celebrating this, there is SO much more to do.'

As the summer holidays approached, Marcus stood up and spoke out again, sending a public letter to all the MPs in Parliament.

'Please reconsider your decision to cancel the food voucher scheme,' he wrote with passion and understanding. 'This is England in 2020, and this is an issue that needs urgent assistance.'

Marcus' amazing message spread far and wide

through social media, calling on the Prime Minister, Boris Johnson, to act. And it worked! Just one day after his letter, the government announced a new summer food fund for vulnerable children, worth over £120 million.

Although Marcus was the hero of the hour, he was too humble to take the credit.

'Just look at what we can do when we come together,' he told his fans. 'THIS is England in 2020.'

Manchester United

🏆 FA Cup: 2015–16

🏆 League Cup: 2016–17

🏆 UEFA Europa League: 2016–17

Individual

🏆 Manchester United Young Player of the Year: 2015–16

🏆 Premier League Player of the Month: January 2019

RASHFORD

(10) THE FACTS

NAME: Marcus Rashford

DATE OF BIRTH: 31 October 1997

AGE: 22

PLACE OF BIRTH: Wythenshawe, Manchester

NATIONALITY: England

BEST FRIEND: Jesse Lingard

CURRENT CLUB: Manchester United

POSITION: ST

THE STATS

Height (cm):	185
Club appearances:	201
Club goals:	64
Club trophies:	3
International appearances:	38
International goals:	10
International trophies:	0
Ballon d'Ors:	0

★ ★ ★ **HERO RATING: 86** ★ ★ ★

GREATEST MOMENTS

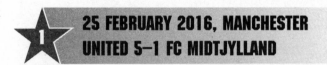

Due to a late injury to Anthony Martial, Marcus was thrown straight into the United starting line-up for this Europa League second leg match. And at the age of eighteen, he took his chance amazingly well. Marcus played the full ninety minutes, scoring two goals and causing all kinds of problems with his speed and movement. A new star was born at Old Trafford.

20 MARCH 2016, MANCHESTER CITY 0–1 MANCHESTER UNITED

Marcus's incredible first month of first-team football continued with this big Manchester derby. City were the team to beat and United did just that, thanks to a great goal from their new young superstar. Marcus used his speed and skill to beat Martín Demichelis and then calmly shoot past Joe Hart. After only eight games, he was already a United hero.

3 JULY 2018, COLOMBIA 1–1 ENGLAND (WON ON PENALTIES!)

Although Marcus only came on for the last seven minutes of this World Cup Round of 16 match, he still played his part. Manager Gareth Southgate needed his coolest, calmest heads for the penalty shoot-out, and Marcus was certainly one of those. With the pressure on, he went second for England, striking the ball confidently into the bottom corner. Ice-cold!

6 MARCH 2019, PSG 1–3 MANCHESTER UNITED

Kylian who? Marcus went head-to-head with Mbappé in the Champions League Round of 16 and came out on the winning side. He gave PSG defender Thilo Kehrer a game to forget, setting one goal up for Romelu Lukaku and then scoring the winner from the penalty spot in the last nail-biting seconds. Once again, Marcus had shown that he was a big game player.

30 OCTOBER 2019, CHELSEA 1–2 MANCHESTER UNITED

On the night before his twenty-second birthday, Marcus proved himself to be United's new star striker. After giving his team the lead with a first-half penalty, he then won the game with a beautiful, swerving free kick from thirty-five yards out. And from that day onwards, Marcus just couldn't stop scoring, reaching nineteen goals by January.

PLAY LIKE YOUR HEROES

THE MARCUS RASHFORD PENALTY ROUTINE

STEP 1: Use your super-speed to race into the opposition box, whether it's you on the ball or one of your teammates. You never know what might happen next…

STEP 2: …PENALTY! As soon as the referee points to the spot, grab the ball and tuck it under your arm. It's yours; don't let anyone take it away from you.

STEP 3: Place it down carefully on the spot, taking a quick look up at the target. Yep, it's still there!

STEP 4: When the referee blows his whistle, take four little shuffles across to the left (that's if you're right-footed, by the way).

STEP 5: Then run forward towards the ball, taking short, stuttering steps to try to fool the keeper.

STEP 6: BANG! Make sure you strike the ball with lots of power, and lots of accuracy too. Aiming for a bottom corner is always best.

STEP 7: GOAL! Keep your celebrations classy and cool, unless, of course, you've just scored a last-minute winner in the Champions League.

TEST YOUR KNOWLEDGE

QUESTIONS

1. Who scored a hat-trick when Marcus went to watch his first-ever Manchester United match?

2. Name at least two other United players who started out at Fletcher Moss Rangers.

3. What did Marcus's brother, Dwaine, do when he first signed for United, aged nine?

4. Marcus used to sneak into the gym to watch which United player practising?

5. Which older United academy players invited Marcus to improve his skills in 'The Cage'?

6. Which Manchester United manager gave Marcus his first team debut?

7. What club trophy did Marcus win at the end of his sensational first season?

8. Marcus played for the England senior team before he played for the Under-21s – true or false?

9. Which three shirt numbers has Marcus worn for Manchester United?

10. Which Manchester United manager helped Marcus to become a better finisher?

11. Which country did Marcus score twice against in the 2018–19 UEFA Nations League?

Answers below. . . No cheating!

1. *The Brazilian Ronaldo (for Real Madrid)* **2.** *Any of Wes Brown, Jesse Lingard, Danny Welbeck and Ravel Morrison* **3.** *He passed his driving test and bought a car so that he could drive Marcus to training!* **4.** *Cristiano Ronaldo* **5.** *Paul Pogba, Jesse Lingard and Ravel Morrison* **6.** *Louis van Gaal* **7.** *The FA Cup* **8.** *True! In the one match he played for the Under-21s after Euro 2016, he scored a hat-trick!* **9.** *39, 19 and 10* **10.** *Ole Gunnar Solskjær* **11.** *Spain*

DELE ALLI

TABLE OF CONTENTS

CHAPTER 1 – **HOMETOWN HERO** 177

CHAPTER 2 – **CREATING CHAOS AT HEELANDS COURTS** . 182

CHAPTER 3 – **CITY COLTS** 187

CHAPTER 4 – **STEVIE G AND BIKES FOR GOALPOSTS** . . . 193

CHAPTER 5 – **MOVING TO MK DONS** 198

CHAPTER 6 – **A NICE NEW HOME WITH THE HICKFORDS** . 202

CHAPTER 7 – **SIZE AND SKILL** 207

CHAPTER 8 – **TRAINING WITH THE FIRST TEAM** 213

CHAPTER 9 – **TWO DARING DEBUTS** 219

CHAPTER 10 – **REGULAR STARTER AT SEVENTEEN** 225

CHAPTER 11 – **MANCHESTER UNITED MASTERCLASS** 232

CHAPTER 12 – **POCHETTINO IMPRESSED** 239

CHAPTER 13 – **LEAVING LEAGUE ONE ON A HIGH** 246

CHAPTER 14 – **PREMIER LEAGUE? NO PROBLEM!** 253

CHAPTER 15 – **ENGLAND'S EXCITING NEW STAR** 260

CHAPTER 16 – **LOSING OUT TO LEICESTER** 267

CHAPTER 17 – **ANOTHER LEARNING EXPERIENCE AT
                EURO 2016** 275

CHAPTER 18 – **DELE THE DESTROYER** 282

CHAPTER 19 – **BIG GOALS AGAINST THE BEST** 290

CHAPTER 20 – **WORLD CUP 2018** 297

CHAPTER 21 – **EUROPEAN EXCITEMENT** 309

CHAPTER 22 – **CHAMPIONS LEAGUE HIGHS AND LOWS** . . 318

CHAPTER 23 – **NEW MOTIVATION FROM MOURINHO** 327

CHAPTER 1

HOMETOWN HERO

26 September 2018, Stadium MK

It felt good to be back. Three years after his big
transfer to Tottenham, Dele was returning to
Stadium MK, the place where his amazing football
adventure had started. He was returning as a Premier
League star and Spurs captain. His manager, Mauricio
Pochettino, had given him the armband for his
special homecoming.

Dele wouldn't be playing against his old club
MK Dons, however. No – Tottenham were taking
on Watford in the Carabao Cup. But while their
new stadium was being built, they had to play their

home games elsewhere. Usually, that was Wembley, which wasn't available for this match. So, for one night only, Dele was back home, kicking off in Milton Keynes.

As he led the Tottenham players out onto the pitch, Dele's mind was filled with many happy memories of Stadium MK:

His first goal against Cambridge City,

His first hat-trick against Crewe Alexandra,

Thrashing the mighty Manchester United 4–0,

And finally, winning promotion to the Championship.

Despite Dele's many achievements since then, that League One runners-up trophy was still the only one that he had ever lifted as a professional player. Hopefully, however, he was going to make the Carabao Cup his second piece of silverware.

Fortunately, the first big chance of the game fell to… Dele! After spreading a lovely ball out wide to Serge Aurier, he sprinted towards the six-yard box, as he loved to do.

'Yes!' Dele called out.

But instead, Serge passed to Lucas Moura, who swivelled and fired the ball across goal. It flew all the way through to the back post, but for once, Dele wasn't quite quick enough to react.

'Nooooo!' he sighed. What a chance to be a home-town hero again!

Never mind, there would be more chances to come. With fifteen minutes to go, Tottenham were losing 1–0, and on their way out of the Carabao Cup. But Dele couldn't let that happen, especially not on his special night as team captain.

So when Érik Lamela passed him the ball, Dele drove powerfully into the box, with only one thing on his mind – scoring a goal. But as he took a second touch, he was tripped by a Watford defender. *Penalty!*

There was no Harry Kane in the Tottenham team that day, so Dele stepped up to take it himself. Pressure? What pressure?! He had no doubt that he would score. With a deep breath and a short run-up, Dele swung his right leg at the ball. The keeper dived the right way, but the spot-kick landed safely in the bottom corner. *1–1!*

Goooooooooooooooooooooaaaaaaaaaaaaaaaalllllllllllll llllllllllllllll!!!!!!!!!!!!!!!!!!!!

'Yesssss!' Dele roared, looking up at the sky and then up at the celebrating Spurs supporters.

He wasn't a true hometown hero yet, though, not unless Tottenham won. Érik gave them a 2–1 lead, but then in the last minute, Watford equalised. There would be no extra-time; the match went straight to penalties.

Dele would take one, of course, but he didn't go first. Instead, he went fourth, once the expectations were even higher. By then, Son Heung-min, Érik and Fernando Llorente had all already scored for Spurs. And their keeper, Paulo Gazzaniga, had already made two super saves to deny Étienne Capoue and Domingos Quina.

So this was it: Dele's chance to win it for Tottenham and show that he was still a hometown hero. After placing the ball down on the spot, Dele took two big steps back, keeping his eyes focused on the target. He wasn't afraid of anything, especially not match-winning moments like this.

Again, he aimed low for the bottom left corner, and again the keeper couldn't stop it. *GOAL!* Tottenham had won 4–2 on penalties – they were through to the next round!

'Nice one, mate!' Érik shouted as they high-fived happily.

Dele played it cool as he turned away to celebrate, but inside he was buzzing with pride and joy. On his emotional return to Stadium MK, he had scored two spot-kicks to win the tie for Spurs.

After shaking hands with all the Watford players, Dele walked around the pitch, clapping for the fans. Most had come from Tottenham, but some were locals who had bought tickets to welcome back their boy wonder.

'Thank you!' he called out to the crowd.

No matter how many Premier League, Champions League and World Cup matches he played in, Dele would always be that kid from Milton Keynes with the mischievous grin.

CHAPTER 2

CREATING CHAOS AT HEELANDS COURTS

'Look who's back, lads!' one of the men called out during a drinks break at Heelands Courts. Together, the footballers turned and watched as a little boy walked determinedly through the council estate and up to the court. 'Wow, he's brave, I'll give him that.'

'Good to see you again, kid!' one of the players said with a smile as the boy entered the cage. 'Ready for Round Two?'

Dele nodded eagerly.

'Great, we thought we might have scared you off after last time!' joked another.

Dele shook his head very seriously. No way, it would take a lot more than some big, strong men to scare him. Especially when it came to playing his new favourite game – football.

Karl, one of the captains, clapped his hands. 'Okay, same teams as before, but we'll take …sorry, what's your name again?'

'Dele,' the boy replied. 'Dele Alli.'

'That's right – Dele's on our team. Right, shall we get started again?'

Suddenly, Karl seemed to remember that he was a responsible adult, even on the football court. 'Wait, your family does know where you are, right?' he asked.

Again, Dele nodded his head eagerly. It was only a half-lie – his mum, Denise, did know that he was outside playing somewhere around the council estate, just not *exactly* where. She wouldn't mind, though; in fact, she'd be pleased. Because if Dele was on the football court, that meant that he was getting some exercise *and* staying out of trouble.

His dad had moved away when Dele was only a baby, leaving him to live with his mum, half-brother and two half-sisters in Bradwell, Milton Keynes.

It was a busy household and a difficult place to be sometimes. So even at the age of seven, Dele was already used to doing his own thing and looking after himself. That's why he was there at Heelands Courts, about to play another game of football against big, strong men.

'Yes, pass it!' Dele called out confidently after running into space.

When he had first started playing, his teammates had just ignored him, but now they trusted him with the ball.

Dele controlled it with the side of his right trainer, all the while looking and listening to the sights and sounds around him.

'Back to me, mate!'

'Over here, Dele!'

'Come on, close the kid down!'

When he had first started playing, his opponents had gone easy on him, but now they treated him like any other player. That was a sign of respect, especially for a seven-year-old boy. It showed that they believed he had the toughness *and* the talent to compete.

However, that respect made it much harder for him. Dele knew that if he took too long on the ball, the other team would use their superior size and strength to swoop in and tackle him. And his own teammates would not be happy about that at all.

Dele had to either play a simple pass or do something special. Those were his two options, but which one would he choose? He knew that his teammates wanted him to keep things simple and safe, but the more he played, the more confident he felt, and the more fun he wanted to have.

Entertainment – that's what football was all about, right? He loved watching and then teaching himself all the stylish skills he saw out on the court – the tricks, the flicks, the million different ways to beat a defender. They might not work every time, but how would he know unless he gave them a go?

So after faking to pass it, Dele spun and slid the ball straight through the defender's legs. *Nutmeg!*

He carried on running to reach the ball on the other side, but by then, the game had already stopped. With that cheeky bit of skill, Dele had created total chaos at Heelands Courts.

'Woah, Danny, are you alright? That kid just SCHOOLED you there!'

'Mate, check your pockets – I think he just stole your self-respect!'

'Nutmegged by a kid – that's a new low for you, lad!'

'Dele, I hope you're ready for Danny's revenge!'

A cheeky smile spread across Dele's fearless little face. Of course, he was ready for anything.

CHAPTER 3

CITY COLTS

As Dele got a bit older, he decided to leave Heelands Courts behind and travel a bit further in search of football fun. One Sunday morning, he went down to a nearby park to watch his friends play for a local youth team called City Colts.

When he saw the players lining up together as a team, wearing their matching kits, Dele thought to himself, 'Cool, I want to do that too!'

Dele was only eight years old at the time, so he didn't yet understand how club football worked. He hoped that it would be the same as the cage games at Heelands Courts, where he could just turn up and ask:

'Excuse me, can I play please?'

Unfortunately, it wasn't that easy. Mike Walsh, the manager of the City Colts Under-9s, looked at the eager young boy in his tracksuit and frowned.

'Sorry, son, this is a league game,' he explained. 'You have to be registered with the team in order to play.'

Dele nodded glumly but he didn't give up. 'I'm really good at football, I swear!' he pleaded.

The Colts manager liked the boy's self-confidence. 'I'm sure you are, kid! But I'm afraid I still can't let you play – not today anyway. Listen, why don't you come and train with us next week and we'll take a look at your skills?'

Dele nodded again, but this time, a lot less glumly. 'Thanks, see you then!'

By the time the next Colts training session started, Walsh had all but forgotten about that offer. Dele, however, had remembered. He had been thinking about it all week and now he was back and ready to show off his skills.

'Hello again!' the manager welcomed him warmly,

before turning to the rest of the squad. 'We have a new player joining us for training this week… sorry kid, I don't even know your name!'

'Dele,' he replied. 'Dele Alli.'

It was a name that Walsh would never forget. Within minutes, the Colts manager had seen enough to know that Dele was the real deal. Where had he learned to play like that? The boy's touch was brilliant and so was his movement, both with and without the ball. But best of all, was his unique style. For such a young kid, Dele played the game with such confidence and creativity. He loved taking risks and trying new things.

When they played a match, Dele nutmegged the Colts' previous best player, flicked the ball over the next defender's head and then volleyed it in. *GOAL!*

'Wow!' was all Walsh could say on the sidelines. Was there anything that this kid couldn't do? He was watching a future professional footballer; he knew it already.

'You were right,' Walsh said with a smile at the end of that first training session. 'You are *REALLY* good at football. I'm very glad you came back today!'

A fearless little grin spread across Dele's little face. 'Me too, Coach!' He couldn't wait to start playing for his new team.

Playing for City Colts wasn't just about being good at football, however. It was also about a sense of belonging and working together as part of a team. Walsh was a manager who cared about his youngsters. He wanted to help them develop as players but also as people. He now knew what Dele was like on the pitch, but what about off the pitch?

Walsh learnt more about his new superstar when he started picking him up and dropping him off after training. Dele told him about the cage matches at Heelands Courts against bigger, older boys:

'So, that's where those skills come from – and that toughness!'

Walsh saw signs of the boy's sometimes difficult home life in Bradwell. It all made the Colts manager realise that he had to handle his promising young player with care.

Most of the time, it was all happiness and trophies. With Dele as their new Number 10, the Colts became almost unbeatable. He had the magical ability to win matches on his own, dribbling his way through whole teams as if it was the easiest thing in the world.

GOAL!

ASSIST!

GOAL!

At times, however, it was all *too* easy for him. And if a match wasn't much of a challenge, then Dele would try to create new challenges for himself. In one game, he even jumped onto the ball and tried to balance there for as long as possible!

'Any more showboating like that and I'll have to send you off,' the referee warned him.

'Sorry!'

With Walsh's help, Dele was becoming a better team player, but he still didn't always like being told what to do. Sometimes, there were strops and sulks at training, which led to time-outs on the sidelines.

'Why can't I just play the way I like to play?'

'No, I don't want to do that. You can't make me!'

But those grumpy moods never lasted long. In no time, Dele would be back out on the pitch again, doing what he did best – playing stylish football with with a big grin on his face.

CHAPTER 4

STEVIE G AND BIKES
FOR GOALPOSTS

'The ball falls to Gerrard, who strikes it first time
from distance, *BANG!...*'

With those words, Dele fired off a shot that flew
past the keeper and just missed the bike that they
were using as a goalpost, in the local car park that
they were pretending was Wembley.

'...*GOOOOOAAAAALLLLL!*'

Dele celebrated by patting the back of his jacket,
right where his name would be on a proper, Premier
League football shirt. That's what Steven Gerrard
had done after scoring a spectacular late equaliser
for Liverpool against West Ham in the 2006 FA Cup

Final. Dele had watched the YouTube clip so many times that he knew it off by heart.

'He's done it...' he called out just like the commentator in the video, '...STEVEN GERRARD!'

'Yeah, well how many Premier League titles has he won then, mate?' jeered the grumpy Manchester United fan in goal as he jogged over to get the ball back.

'Whatever, Stevie's won the Champions League!'

The Liverpool and England midfielder had quickly become Dele's biggest football hero. They played in slightly different positions – Dele was more of an attacking Number 10, whereas Stevie was a box-to-box Number 8. They also had slightly different playing styles – Dele was more about silky skills, whereas Stevie was more about perfect passing. But ultimately, Dele felt like they had lots in common. For example:

1) They both enjoyed every part of the game – passing, shooting and dribbling, but also heading and tackling too. For City Colts, Dele was always chasing back to reclaim the ball with crunching challenges.

He wanted to be involved in everything, at both ends of the pitch.

2) They both loved assists almost as much as goals. Despite his awesome skills, Dele wasn't a selfish attacker. He played with his head up, looking for ways to connect with the strikers. In club football, Dele had learnt that he couldn't just show off his new tricks all the time like he did at Heelands Courts; that didn't win you games, tournaments or league titles.

And best of all:

3) They were both brave, big game players. Another one of Dele's favourite YouTube videos was Liverpool's legendary second-half comeback against AC Milan in the 2005 Champions League Final. And who had started it off, with a brilliant header and then a 'Make Some Noise!' signal to the supporters? Stevie G – what a hero! FA Cup Finals, Champions League Finals, World Cups – no matter how important the match was, he just played the same way he always did, with drive and determination.

'I'm the same!' Dele thought to himself.

Stevie didn't fear any opponent, and neither did Dele. He believed in himself and his ability to beat anyone. With the ball at his feet, he felt unstoppable. Because thanks to all those hours spent in the cage at Heelands Courts, he knew hundreds of different ways to dribble past defenders and score great goals. All he had to was pick which one to go for.

When City Colts needed a match-winning moment of magic, they turned to Dele, and he usually delivered. He had that strong character, that 'I'm not afraid of anything' attitude, on top of his tremendous football talent. What a winning combination! Walsh was right; one day, Dele could play in the Premier League, and maybe even for England, just like his hero, Stevie G. Why not?

The only thing that could stop Dele from achieving that dream was himself. Unfortunately, when he wasn't playing for the Colts or having a kickaround in the car park with bikes for goalposts, he had started hanging around with the wrong crowd.

In Bradwell, it was often difficult for a young boy like Dele to ignore the bad influences around him.

He knew kids in local gangs, who were already involved in crime. For now, though, football was keeping Dele focused on the right path. If he wasn't careful, however, he could end up making bad mistakes and wasting his tremendous talent. Luckily, he had people around him who wouldn't let that happen. Instead, they helped him to make the most of himself, and follow in Stevie G's footsteps.

CHAPTER 5

MOVING TO MK DONS

In Milton Keynes, 2004 turned out to be a big year for football. While Dele was starting his career at City Colts, just a few miles down the road, MK Dons were starting life as a League One club.

The team formerly known as 'Wimbledon' already played their home games in the town at Stadium MK, but now that they had just been relegated from the Championship, the owners decided that it was time for bigger changes. So, for the new season, the club had a new name as well as a new division to play in.

Exciting times! But while Dele was soon winning tournaments with the Colts, the MK Dons didn't get off to such a good start. In fact, in 2006, the club dropped down into League Two. What a disappointment, both for the Dons and for the town of Milton Keynes!

That same year, however, MK made a very wise decision for the future of their football club. They hired a new youth coach: Mark Walsh, the City Colts manager. And which young superstar did he take with him to his new team? Yes, that's right – Dele!

'It's only a trial at first,' Walsh explained to his ten-year-old wonderkid, 'but I'm sure you'll find a way to impress the other coaches.'

Wow, this was it; Dele's first chance to play at a professional football academy. He couldn't wait for his new challenge to begin. After two weeks of the trial, everything was going according to plan. Dele was playing well and there hadn't been any real sulks or strops. So far. But as the Under-11s prepared for a friendly against Chelsea at Stamford Bridge, Walsh had some bad news for Dele – he wouldn't be able to play in the game.

'What? Why not?!'

All Dele wanted to do was play football – what was wrong with that? It felt so unfair that he had to miss the team's biggest match of the season, just because he was new and not a permanent player yet. Rubbish! It was like that first Sunday morning at City Colts all over again. Before he could control himself, Dele exploded with hurt and anger. 'Fine, I'm done here, and I'm not coming back!'

It took Walsh a lot of time and effort but eventually, he did persuade Dele to come back and play for the MK Dons again. And once he started training four times a week with the club, he calmed down, worked hard and just got better and better and better. It was a joy to watch a kid playing with such confidence and creativity.

'Brilliant through-ball, Dele – you created that chance out of nothing!'

'Well done, lad – that's top work there!'

It certainly helped that Walsh had worked with him before and so knew how best to handle him. Sometimes, Dele needed a bit of detailed, one-to-one coaching, and sometimes he needed his own space to develop his game naturally. Sometimes, he needed an arm around his shoulder, and sometimes he needed an angry time-out.

But most importantly, Dele always needed to be challenged on the football field. If things became too easy, he just got bored. So, every week, Walsh tried to raise the bar a bit higher for him: more goals, more assists, and even more ideas.

'What else do you think you could have done in that position?'

'Erm... play the pass out wide and then make a late run into the box?'

'Good, try that next time.'

Like his hero, Stevie G, Dele had that drive and determination to keep learning and improving. Now that he was a rising star at the MK Dons academy, he was fully focused on football and making the most of his talent. Dele could see a successful career ahead of him, and nothing was going to distract him from achieving his goals.

CHAPTER 6

A NICE NEW HOME WITH THE HICKFORDS

Dele was really loving his new life at the MK Dons academy. What was there not to love about it? He was having loads of fun, playing loads of football, and hanging out with his new friends.

'This is the life, lads!' Dele joked at training. 'Football all day every day!'

Yes, the Under-14s were like a band of brothers, both on and off the pitch. They all got on really well and that showed in their excellent match-day performances. Although there were a lot of promising young players in the squad, they never saw the academy as a talent contest. No, they weren't competing against each other. Instead, there

was a real team spirit because they were all trying to
make it to the top together, including:

A fast forward called George Williams,

A big centre-back called Brendan Galloway,

A dogged defender called Harry Hickford,

And a midfield magician called Dele Alli.

They were all good friends, but Dele and Harry
were *BEST* friends. They clicked straight away and
soon they were inseparable. Not only did they play
for the same team, but they also went to the same
school, The Radcliffe. They spent every day together,
talking endlessly about their favourite thing –
football, of course!

'Here they are – attached at the hip, as always.
Come on, let's go, Tweedledum and Tweedledee!'

Harry's parents, Alan and Sally, got to know their
son's best friend very well. They knew that things
were difficult for Dele at home, so they kindly took
him to the MK Dons matches and then often invited
him home for dinner afterwards. Before long, Dele
started staying over after dinner, and then he started
staying there three days a week, then four, then

five... He was part of the Hickford family now and he was hardly going home to Bradwell at all.

'We've been thinking,' Harry's parents said to Dele one day when he was thirteen years old. 'How would you feel about coming to live here permanently? We'll need to check with your mum first, of course, but we'd love to have you and we've got the room if that's what you want.'

'Wow, really?'

Dele was delighted – it was definitely what he wanted. He had been hoping that they would ask him for ages. He loved living with the Hickfords in the nice neighbourhood of Cosgrove, but what about his mum back in Bradwell?

For Dele's mum, Denise, it wasn't easy to let Dele go, but she knew that it was the best thing for him. If he stayed, she would always worry about her son getting into trouble like some of the other kids on their estate. Alan and Sally were good people, who would look after Dele and offer him a safe environment. That was the most important thing for him and for his future football career. The

Hickfords' house was only six miles away, but that was still far enough to leave the bad influences in Bradwell behind.

'Well, I guess we really are brothers now!' Harry said with a smile as he helped Dele move in the last of his belongings.

Dele smiled. 'Yeah, and I'm two months older than you, so don't forget that!'

Now that they lived together, they could start plotting their path all the way to the MK Dons first team.

'In a couple of years, we could be playing for the Under-18s, and then if we do well, we'll get called up to the Reserves, and then League One, here we come!'

At the end of the 2008–09 season, the Dons had won promotion from League Two at last. They had achieved that under the guidance of ex-Chelsea star Roberto Di Matteo, but now the former Manchester United midfielder Paul Ince was their manager again, with Karl Robinson as his assistant.

The most exciting thing for Dele and Harry,

though, was that the club was calling up more and more of their most talented youth players. Sam Baldock had made the move from the academy to the first team in 2007 and now he was their star striker. After that, many more followed: Adam Chicksen, Tom Flanagan, David King, Daniel Powell, and Sam's brother, George Baldock.

'And we'll be next!' MK Dons' brand-new 'brothers' declared confidently.

As he settled into his nice new home with the Hickfords, Dele felt more determined than ever to achieve his dream of becoming a professional footballer.

CHAPTER 7

SIZE AND SKILL

Even in that talented MK Dons youth team, Dele still stood out head and shoulders above the rest. It was clear to anyone watching that he was a truly special player with truly special skills. On the ball, he could do things that the others didn't even dream of.

A scoop pass to a striker – *Olé!*

A flick over a midfielder's head – *Olé!*

A nutmeg through a defender's legs – *Olé!*

A back-heel shot past a goalkeeper – *Olé!*

'That kid's not afraid to try anything, is he?' laughed the Dons' youth team director, Mike Dove, full of admiration.

To some, it might have looked like arrogance, but

it wasn't really. It was just Dele's unique combination of confidence and creativity. He played football for fun and without fear. He backed himself to find a way out of any tricky situation, any tight space on the pitch. His head was full of new ideas and if a trick failed the first time, he didn't just give up on it. No, he would try it again and again until it worked perfectly. Dele had first developed his skills playing street football back at Heelands Courts, and now he was taking them to the next level at MK Dons.

'If we coach him well, that kid could become a real superstar!' thought the Under-15s manager, Dan Micciche.

However, Dele's arrival coincided with his reaching a difficult age. Suddenly, all the kids around him were growing taller and stronger – everyone except him. And if you were thirteen years old, football wasn't just about your skill anymore; it was also about your size.

That meant Dele was at a big disadvantage. Now, when he tried to dribble past defenders like normal, they could just push him off the ball.

'Hey!' Dele protested, but the referee shook his head. 'No foul – play on!'

With every minute, Dele was getting more and more frustrated up front. He wanted to be on the ball all the time, trying out his usual tricks, but that was impossible when his opponents kept barging him out of the way!

'Ref!'

What was he supposed to do when he was so much smaller? The good old days of street skills were officially over; Dele needed to find a new way to win matches for MK Dons, and fast. It was size that seemed to matter most, so why wasn't he growing big and strong like everyone else?

'Don't worry, your time will come,' Micciche tried to reassure him.

'Okay, but when?'

Dele didn't want to wait around. His best friends Harry and George had both already had their growth spurts and now they'd been called up to Under-16s. They were on their way to the first team without him! Football just wasn't as much fun anymore.

Micciche could see that Dele wasn't happy. He had lost his flair and his fearlessness too. Where was that desire to improve?

'Hey, size isn't everything,' Micciche reminded Dele one day when he was looking particularly miserable at training. Hopefully, some extra motivation would help cheer him up. 'Look at Maradona – he's only five-foot five and and he's one of the greatest footballers of all time! He didn't let his size stop him, did he? No, he just worked on his skills until he could escape from even the biggest, baddest defenders!'

Dele nodded his head, his determination returning. His manager was right; he was too good to just give up now and let big defenders boss him around. He was an intelligent player, with lots and lots of ideas. He could overcome this new challenge.

Until he grew taller and stronger, Dele would just have to work harder to outsmart his opponents and be more creative than ever. For now, he had to forget about what his friends were doing and focus on becoming the best footballer he could be.

'Always think one step ahead, before you even get the ball,' Micciche coached him. 'Pass and move, pass and move. Play it as early as possible – that way, they can't tackle you!'

'Look for that space between their midfield and defence. Keep searching until you find it!'

'And use your pace as well – that's another powerful weapon! Mix it up, with bursts of speed at just the right moment.'

Dele listened carefully and learned quickly. But it was when Micciche moved him into a deeper midfield role, that everything really fell into place. Suddenly, he had that extra bit of time and space to pick his pass or create some magic. Perfect!

By the time Dele turned fifteen, he had become a better footballer and a bigger, stronger one too. All of a sudden, he had shot up to six-foot tall and he wasn't finished growing yet. Hurray! At last, he had the skill *and* the size – surely there was nothing stopping him now.

With a huge 'Thanks!' to Micciche, Dele moved up to join Harry and George in the Under-16s, then the Under-17s, and then the Under-18s…

…Because Dele was back and better than ever!
Once again, he was the top young talent that the
whole club was talking about. Before long, word had
spread all the way to Karl Robinson. After one season
as Ince's assistant, he had been named as the new
MK Dons manager in May 2010.

Robinson was on the lookout for promising young
players to promote to the first team. And when he
went to watch Dele play for the first time, he could
hardly contain his excitement.

'Wow, this kid is going be a superstar!' Robinson
boldly predicted.

CHAPTER 8

TRAINING WITH THE FIRST TEAM

It was fortunate that Dele had got his fearlessness back because ahead of the 2011–12 season, Robinson decided to call up three young players to train with the MK Dons first team:

George,

Brendan,

And Dele!

This was an extremely big deal, especially for fifteen-year-olds. Were they really ready for this? They would be boys amongst men! As they arrived at the training ground, George and Brendan both looked a bit nervous, but not Dele. He had a mischievous grin on his face as usual.

He was determined to make an unforgettable first impression...

When the three youngsters entered the dressing room, the senior players stopped talking and turned to look.

'Great, some more shy, quiet kids to play against!' thought Darren Potter, the experienced Dons midfielder.

Darren had seen it so many times before: talented young players who turned up at training with the first team but were too worried about making mistakes to actually do anything impressive. Then after a few awkward sessions, they disappeared back to the academy.

Well, that's what usually happened at MK Dons, but Darren was about to meet a different kind of talent. Dele wasn't going to change his game just because he was training with the big boys now. This was his chance to prove himself on the pitch, like at Heelands Courts all over again. Confidence and creativity had got him this far, and now these qualities would get him into the first team too. So, in the first few minutes, when Darren came over to tackle him, Dele coolly slid it straight through his legs. *Nutmeg!*

Woooooaaaaah! Had the new kid really just embarrassed an experienced pro like that? Where was the respect? There was stunned silence all over the field. Dele carried on playing, as if it was nothing special, but he knew that his plan had worked. The senior players had certainly noticed him now.

'That boy is BRAVE!' was their first thought, but as the session went on, they added an extra bit:

'And BRILLIANT!'

After that first cheeky nutmeg, Dele didn't switch to keeping things safe and simple. No, he carried on showing off his full range of skills. A flick pass here, a back-heel there, a dribble between two defenders to score. *GOAL!*

So this was the new wonderkid that everyone was talking about – he was making professional footballers look like fools! Well, it was time to see whether the boy could cope with a bit of physicality.

A push here, a shirt-pull there, a crunching challenge from behind. *FOUL!*

Dele didn't complain and he didn't back down. He just picked himself up off the grass each time and carried on fighting for the ball. It would take more than a few strong tackles to scare him.

As Robinson watched from the sidelines, a big smile spread across his face. Talent? Tick! Toughness? Tick! Yes, Dele definitely had something special about him. And with a few more years of development, he would be ready to become a superstar.

During the 2011–12 season, Dele didn't quite get to make his debut for the MK Dons first team, but he trained with the squad regularly, and he was a sub for all of their FA Cup matches. That turned out to be an exciting, but also frustrating experience. The good news was that he got his very own shirt number – 36 – and the chance to feel like part of the first team. The bad news was that Dele had to do two of his least favourite things in football – watching and waiting.

When the Dons went 5–0 up in the First

Round against Nantwich Town, Robinson turned to his youngsters on the bench. He still had two substitutions left to make…

'Pick me! Pick me!' Dele muttered under his breath, moving his legs around restlessly.

But instead, Robinson decided to bring on George and then Brendan. Noooo! When George scored a sixth goal in the ninetieth minute, Dele was pleased for his friend, but he couldn't hide his own disappointment.

'That could have been me!' he thought to himself.

Sadly, there was no space for youngsters in their Second Round win at Barnet, or in their Third Round defeat to QPR.

Oh well, Dele's MK Dons debut would definitely come soon – during the next season for sure. Until then, he just had to keep working hard in training, and show Robinson that he was ready to shine brightly for the first team.

One day, the players were practising a new corner routine. As the cross came in, it was Dele's job to make a run to the front post and jump up to get the flick-on.

'Right, let's give it a go!' Robinson called out, clapping his hands together.

But as Dele made his move towards the front post, he could see that the cross was coming in at the wrong height for a header. Never mind, he would just have to use his incredible creativity. After all, he had the confidence to try anything. In a flash, he turned his body and volleyed the ball into the net with the heel of his boot. *GOAL!*

Extraordinary! As everyone stared at him in disbelief, Dele decided to celebrate by performing a second skills show with his chewing gum. He juggled it:

From one knee, to the other knee,

Then from the right foot, to the left foot,

And then for a finale, he flicked it up and caught it in his mouth again. *Ta-da!*

'Mate, that's disgusting!' George joked as they got ready to try the corner routine again.

'I think what you mean is – that's different class!' Dele replied with a cheeky grin on his face.

CHAPTER 9

TWO DARING DEBUTS

A year on from that disappointing day at Nantwich Town, Dele was back on the bench for MK Dons in the FA Cup First Round. This time, they were playing Cambridge City and Dele had the number 21 on his back, plus Harry and Brendan there to keep him company.

'Let's hope we thrash them,' they agreed as the game kicked off, 'because then we might get some game-time at the end!'

But as the second half went on, the score stayed at 0–0, and Robinson started to wonder what changes he should make...

'Pick me! Pick me!' Dele muttered, moving his legs around restlessly again.

His hopes were a lot higher for this match. He was sixteen now and he was one of only two attackers on the MK Dons bench: the other was the former Leeds United and Manchester United forward, Alan Smith, who was now more of a central midfielder. So, if the manager wanted a match-winning moment of magic, then Dele was his man.

'Alli, get ready,' he heard one of the coaches call out, 'you're coming on!'

At last, Dele's MK Dons debut had arrived! With a quick 'Good luck!' high-five from his friends, he made his way down to the touchline.

Substitution for MK Dons. Replacing Number 23 Jay O'Shea, Number 21 Dele Alli…

'Who? Who?' the Cambridge City fans jeered.

Dele had about thirty minutes to prove himself and make sure that they remembered his name. As he ran onto the field, he didn't feel nervous at all. Why would he? He was playing first-team football for the first time! This wasn't something to worry about; this was fun and exciting.

'Yes, over here!' Dele cried out, racing into space. He wanted to be on the ball as much as possible.

And when it came to him, what next? Well, Dele wasn't interested in playing safe, simple passes. What was the point of that? So instead, his very first touch was a back-heel.

'What was that?!' On the touchline, Robinson looked like he was ready to tear his hair out. A back-heel? What did the boy think he was doing – having a casual kickaround with his mates? The Dons weren't winning 6–0; they were drawing 0–0 against a non-league team! If Dele didn't start taking it seriously, he would be back on the bench...

The next time the ball came to him, Dele fooled the defender by letting it roll across his body, and onto his stronger right foot.

'Yes, yes, yes!' Robinson thought, his excitement building.

Dele could hear two teammates calling for the pass but instead, he decided to go for goal on his debut, from thirty yards out. Why not? He believed in himself.

'No, no, no!' Robinson groaned as Dele pulled his leg back and unleashed the shot. Luckily, it took a deflection and went out for a corner, because otherwise he would have been in big trouble with his manager.

Once he had calmed down a little, Robinson couldn't help admiring his young player's confidence. Nothing fazed Dele, not even making his first-team debut at the age of sixteen. When it came to football, the kid was totally fearless.

By the time the final whistle blew, Dele had shown more flashes of his bravery and brilliance, but it wasn't enough to change the score line of 0–0. The Dons would have to do better in the replay back at Stadium MK.

And Dele would have the chance to do better on his full debut. Yes, Robinson had seen enough in those thirty minutes to think that his young star was ready to play from the start. So when the teamsheet was revealed, there was his name and number – '21 ALLI'

– alongside Stephen Gleeson in central midfield.

'Good luck!' his manager told him before kick-off. 'Don't let me down.'

And Dele didn't. He played with the determination of a sixteen-year-old, combined with the composure of an experienced pro. With his help, the Dons dominated the game and put in a much-improved performance. They were 3–0 up by half-time and late in the second half, he even scored a stunning strike to complete a fantastic full debut.

When Dean Lewington passed the ball to him, Dele was at least thirty-five yards away from goal. It would have to be an absolute beauty to beat the keeper from there, but why not? It was worth a hit. For him, nothing felt impossible. This time, the Dons were winning 4–1, so he knew that his manager wouldn't mind. Dele shifted it onto his right foot and *BANG!* The ball flew through the air like an arrow, past the Cambridge City defenders and all the way into the top corner of the net. *5–1!*

Goooooooooooooooooooooaaaaaaaaaaaaaaaaalllllllllll llllllllllllllllll!!!!!!!!!!!!!!!!!!!

'Wow!' marvelled the 4,000 supporters at Stadium MK that night.

Dele started jogging back to the halfway line as if it was no big deal, but his teammates weren't going to let him get away without a proper celebration.

'What a worldie!'

'Congrats, kid!'

'You won't score a better one than that, mate!'

'Stevie G, eat your heart out!'

They cheered, wrapping a delighted Dele in a big group hug.

What a proud moment – the first of many great goals, hopefully! It felt like the start of something really special.

And Robinson, the MK Dons manager, agreed. On the bench, he smiled and turned to his coaches. 'What did I tell you? That kid is going to be a superstar!'

CHAPTER 10

REGULAR STARTER AT SEVENTEEN

After his cracker against Cambridge City, Dele went on to make five more first-team appearances across all competitions. He wanted to play for MK Dons every week, of course, but he didn't mind waiting as long as he was moving in the right direction.

'Dele's a very special player,' Robinson told the media at the end of the 2012–13 season. 'He's going to go right to the top of English football and we've just got to make sure we nurture him in the right way.'

So, did that mean Dele would get to play fifteen matches next year? Or maybe even twenty? That might have been the plan at first, but not after Dele's phenomenal preseason. While other players were slowly getting back in shape after their summer holidays, he was looking fitter, stronger and fiercer than ever. Whatever challenge the coaches set, he always fought his way to the top. Dele had found a new gear, and now he was unstoppable.

'Man, do you ever stop moving?' Darren panted as he tried his best to mark his young teammate in training. 'You're an absolute machine!'

Dele gave his most mischievous grin. 'Come on, keep up – or do you want me to nutmeg you again? Just be glad that we play for the same club, mate!'

Everyone at MK Dons was very impressed with Dele's development – especially their winger, Luke Chadwick who, back in 1999, had been part of Manchester United's amazing Treble-winning squad under Sir Alex Ferguson. Luke had played with Premier League legends like David Beckham, Ryan Giggs and Paul Scholes, and he could see that Dele shared many of the same qualities. The speed, the skill, the desire – but above all, the self-belief. He played with confidence, like he could achieve anything.

'You're not afraid of anyone, are you?' Luke laughed as Dele battled for the ball against Tom, the Don's biggest defender. 'If you can play like that in League One this season, then the top clubs will soon come calling!'

That sounded super exciting, but Dele was taking things one step at a time. For now, he was focused on starring for his local, boyhood team. For a promising young player, MK Dons was the perfect place to be. He could play without pressure, and he was sure to get a lot more game-time there. The club had just given him the Number 14 shirt, a clear sign that he was creeping closer and closer to that First XI.

Ahead of the opening game of the new season, Robinson announced that Dele would be starting alongside Darren and Stephen in midfield. No-one at MK was surprised by that news, not after preseason. Yes, he was still only seventeen, but Dele was a superstar in the making.

'Up you go, kid!' With Darren in a deeper role behind him, Dele had the freedom to get forward as much as possible. He wasn't yet producing magic every week, but the more he played, the more consistent and creative he became. By the time Stevenage arrived at Stadium MK, Dele was looking really dangerous.

With twenty-two minutes played, Patrick Bamford, their striker who was on loan from Chelsea, was already on a hat-trick, and he was on the attack again. This time, though, he looked up and spotted Dele on the left, making a bursting run into the box.

'Yes!' he called out, pointing towards the penalty spot.

At first, Patrick's pass looked a little too heavy, but determined Dele wasn't giving up. He slid across the grass and stretched out his long left leg to bring the ball under control. What next? He didn't have enough time to get back up before a defender closed him down, so instead he took the shot from on the floor. What quick, creative thinking! It wasn't his most powerful strike, but it was enough to catch the keeper out.

Goooooooooooooooooooooaaaaaaaaaaaaaaaaalllllllllllll llllllllllllll!!!!!!!!!!!!!!!!!!!!!

His first league goal! Dele raced over towards the corner flag to celebrate. Soon, he was at the bottom of a big pile of players.

'Next time, can you play a better pass?' Dele joked with Patrick as they jogged back to the centre-circle. They were forming a strong friendship, as well as an excellent strike partnership.

'Nah, next time, I'm taking the shot myself!'

In the second half, Dele won a penalty, which Shaun Williams scored to make it 4–1. When MK's young stars were at their best, they could beat anyone in League One.

Sadly, Patrick's loan spell ended in January, but by then, Dele was ready to make the step up from regular starter to regular scorer.

In the opening minutes against Shrewsbury Town, he chased after Stephen's through-ball and headed it bravely past the keeper. *1–0!*

Away at Notts County, Jordan Spence's long pass bounced down in the boggy penalty area. While the players around him panicked and miskicked, Dele calmly slotted the ball into the bottom corner. *1–0!*

'Nice one, we needed a bit of class there!' their striker Izale McLeod said with a smile.

And early in the second half, Dele was on the scoresheet again. Daniel Powell pounced on a poor back pass, dribbled forward and then played it across to his teenage teammate. *2–0!*

'Cheers, mate!' Dele shouted as he threw his arms out wide. There were only 3,000 fans at Meadow Lane that night, but one day soon, he would be celebrating in front of much bigger crowds.

It was Dele 2, Notts County 0. Could he add a third goal and complete his first professional hat-trick? Yes, he could, with another assist from Daniel. In the last minute, his chipped pass landed at Dele's feet, on the left edge of the penalty area.

In the middle, Izale was calling for the cross, but Dele had a different idea. The final whistle was just seconds away, but he dribbled into the box as if he had all the time in the world. Then with a quick look-up, Dele curled a shot past the keeper, and past the diving defender on the line too.

Goooooooooooooooooooaaaaaaaaaaaaaaaaalllllllllll lllllllllllll!!!!!!!!!!!!!!!!!!!!!

What a moment! His eighteenth birthday was still one month away, and Dele was already a professional hat-trick hero. Unbelievable! With his right arm up high in the air, he raced away to celebrate. He couldn't wait to take that match ball home with him.

'The game's been won by a wonder boy,' Robinson declared afterwards, with no doubt in his mind. 'He's one of the most gifted seventeen-year-olds this country has ever seen.'

Wow – if England's top teams hadn't already heard the name 'Dele Alli', well they definitely had now.

CHAPTER 11

MANCHESTER UNITED MASTERCLASS

26 August 2014, Stadium MK

Although promotion to the Championship was MK Dons' top priority for the 2014–15 season, a fun cup run was always a nice bonus. After beating bitter rivals AFC Wimbledon in the EFL Cup First Round, they now faced one of the most famous clubs in the world – Manchester United.

Oh boy, this was a big one! But Dele didn't feel nervous; he was going to treat it just like any other game. In the Dons dressing room, he went through his same old routine:

Right sock, then right boot (size 10), then right

*shin pad (the same ones he had worn since he
was eleven years old), left sock, then left boot (size
10-and-a-half), then left shin pad...*

Right, he was ready! Ready to raise his game.
Behind that calm, fearless face, Dele couldn't wait
for the most important match of his career so far.
He was already a star in League One; now, this was
the next step, his toughest challenge yet. With the
TV cameras watching, he was determined to prove
himself against top Premier League players.

The new Manchester United manager Louis van
Gaal had decided to rest his biggest stars like
Wayne Rooney, Juan Mata and Robin van Persie,
but there was still plenty of talent in their team.
Their two starting strikers, Danny Welbeck and
Chicharito, had scored over fifty Premier League
goals between them. Goalkeeper David de Gea and
midfielders Anderson and Shinji Kagawa had all
cost about £20 million each, and then there was
Nick Powell, the 'next big thing' United had signed
from League Two club Crewe Alexandra
for £6 million.

'Well, we'll see about that,' Dele thought to himself as the two teams walked out for kick-off.

From his very first touch, Dele took confident control of the game. He passed and moved, passed and moved, all over the pitch. At the age of eighteen, he was putting on a midfield masterclass and United couldn't handle him.

When they tried to get physical, he showed that he could make tough tackles too. *CRUNCH!* Poor Powell wasn't going to forget the day when he first played against Dele Alli. He wasn't afraid of anything or anyone. Jonny Evans tried to outmuscle him in the box, but Dele went shoulder to shoulder with him and came away with the ball.

'Hurray!' the MK Dons fans cheered when their boy wonder won the battle.

Dele was everywhere, enjoying his time in the spotlight. One minute, he was back heading away a United corner, and the next, he was at the other end, taking a long-range shot.

'Unlucky!' Robinson encouraged from the sidelines. 'Keep going!'

Whenever a teammate looked up to play a pass, there was Dele, calling for the ball, with lots of space and time. MK Dons were doing brilliantly; now they just needed to score a goal…

Halfway through the first half, United made a mess of things at the back. As Evans took his time on the ball, Ben Reeves raced in to close him down. Not only did he block the pass, but Ben also then got to the rebound first, cutting it back for Will Grigg to score. *1–0 to MK Dons!*

'Get in!' Dele cheered as he rushed over to celebrate with Will and Ben. The Cup upset was on!

It stayed 1–0 until midway through the second half. By that time, some of the MK players were starting to slow down, and their fans were starting to fear the worst.

Not Dele, though. He wasn't tired and he certainly wasn't scared. With cool confidence, he kept calling for the ball and swapping neat one-twos with his teammates. As much as Dele loved to get forward and attack, Robinson had given him a different, deeper role to play that day. He had to show discipline alongside Darren in the middle and help protect the defence.

'Come on, nothing's getting past us, okay?'

When Evans flicked the ball on into the MK six-yard box, it was Dele who reacted first to hook it away, high into the air. And by the time it eventually dropped, he had rushed out to the edge of the area, to steal the ball from Michael Keane before he could shoot.

'Hurray!' the fans cheered. Was there anything that Dele couldn't do? What an amazing all-round player he was!

As the minutes ticked by, MK Dons just had to hold on, and hope for another Manchester United mistake…

At last, it arrived. On a quick counter-attack, Ben delivered a perfect cross to Will, who somehow chested the ball past De Gea. *2–0!*

Yes! A second goal was just what MK needed to calm things down, and there were even more to come.

Benik Afobe came off the bench to finish off a brilliant team move. *3–0!*

'Yes, mate!' Dele cheered as they did a little dance together by the corner flag.

And then Benik dribbled his way through the United defence to score again. *4–0!*

Wow, what a night, and what a thrashing! And yet even in the very last minute, Dele was still battling for the ball and chasing back to help the defence. His team had a clean sheet to keep. Only when the final whistle blew, did he stop and breathe and punch the air. Job done!

'We just beat Manchester United!' Dele cried out in disbelief.

Benik smiled and shook his head. 'No mate, we just *BATTERED* Manchester United!'

Dele asked to swap shirts with Welbeck, but the striker had already offered it to someone else. Oh well, nothing was going to ruin his night to remember. Although every single Dons player deserved so much credit for an excellent team display, there were some clear, stand-out performances:

Will and Benik, who had both scored two goals each,

Ben, who had grabbed three amazing assists,

And most eye-catching of all,

Dele, the confident young pass master who had outplayed the whole Manchester United midfield.

Back in 2003, United had been battered by another amazing eighteen-year-old – a skilful winger called Cristiano Ronaldo. After that game, Sir Alex Ferguson had signed him to the club straight away. Dele wasn't as lucky, but lots of other big clubs were interested in him.

CHAPTER 12

POCHETTINO IMPRESSED

Among the many football scouts and coaches watching Dele's Manchester United masterclass, was Mauricio Pochettino, the new Tottenham manager. He was so impressed by what he had seen that he went straight to the MK boardroom after the match.

'That kid is incredible,' Pochettino said with a smile. 'I want him in my team!'

It was a former Spurs manager, David Pleat, who had first spotted Dele's potential and recommended him to Pochettino.

'He's really athletic, he runs up and down all game long, and he's strong in the air too,' Pleat wrote in his scouting report. 'Plus, he seems very mature for such a young player.'

Interesting! Tottenham already had a top goal scorer in Harry Kane and a creative playmaker in Christian Eriksen, but what they were still missing was that box-to-box energy in midfield. They needed someone with skill and speed, but also power and determination. And the more that Pochettino watched Dele play, the more he knew that he would be perfect for the role. He knew this because, outside the box, Dele played like a clever midfielder, but once he stepped inside, he became a clinical striker.

After finishing his first full season with seven goals, Dele had set himself much higher targets this time around.

GOAL! A tap-in against Peterborough.

GOAL! A cheeky chip over the keeper at Barnsley.

GOAL! GOAL! GOAL! Another hat-trick for Dele, this time against Crewe – one leaping header and two quality right-foot finishes, plus a beautiful assist for Benik.

'Too easy!' Dele joked with his teammates, but it

was true. He was getting too good for League One now and everyone knew it. Although he had just signed a new contract until 2017, there was no way that Dele would stay that long at MK. It was time for him to test himself at a higher level.

And it was time for Tottenham to make their move before it was too late. Because lots of other clubs were keeping a close eye on Dele, including Aston Villa, Newcastle United, Bayern Munich and his favourite team as a kid, Liverpool. They had even invited Dele to come to Anfield, hoping that a chat with his hero, Steven Gerrard, might persuade him to sign.

'Wow, I'm going to meet Stevie G!' Dele thought excitedly, like he was ten years old again. However, when he arrived at Liverpool, Gerrard was nowhere to be seen.

'Sorry, he's sleeping ahead of our big game tomorrow,' the club explained.

Oh well, never mind – it was still a good chance for Dele to go behind the scenes at one of the biggest clubs in the world. As he looked around, everything looked so massive, modern and amazing, especially compared to MK. It really would be a dream come true to play at a stadium like Anfield, in front of 50,000 fans.

However, as Liverpool paused to think, Tottenham jumped ahead to take the lead. Pochettino had found the box-to-box midfielder that he was looking for, and he didn't want to wait until the summer, and maybe miss out on signing Dele.

'Let's do the deal now,' he told the Spurs chairman, Daniel Levy, during the January transfer window.

When he heard the news, Dele was delighted. A proper offer from a Premier League club? That was his dream come true. 'I'm in!' he told his agent immediately.

'Woah, woah, woah – slow down!' he replied. 'Take your time and think about what you really want.'

Okay, well, Dele wanted to play for a top team, and Tottenham was certainly one of those. They had just finished sixth in the Premier League, which meant they would be playing in Europe too.

Dele also wanted to play for a top manager, who

believed in him and wanted to help him become a better footballer.

For that, he knew Pochettino would be perfect. The Argentinian had a great record of improving players at Southampton – Luke Shaw, Adam Lallana, Morgan Schneiderlin, Calum Chambers, Jay Rodriguez, Dejan Lovren... the list went on and on.

But Dele didn't want to go and sit on the bench at a big club. That would feel like a step backwards after over eighty first-team games for MK Dons by the age of eighteen. He wanted to play as many games as possible. He decided to talk about it with Pochettino.

'Don't worry, I don't see you as a player for the future,' Pochettino promised Dele when they met to discuss the deal. 'If you sign for us, you'll go straight into the Spurs first-team squad. And if you keep working hard and impressing the coaches, then you will get plenty of chances to play.'

Dele nodded his head happily; that was exactly what he wanted to hear. He understood that the Premier League was going to be a big step-up, but he was determined to do his absolute best to shine

straight away. Like MK Dons, Tottenham was a club
that gave their young players plenty of chances –
Ryan Mason, Andros Townsend, and of course,
Harry Kane.

Okay, deal almost done! Dele only had one more
request: 'Can I please go back to MK on loan for the
rest of this season?'

He couldn't leave the Dons just yet, not when
promotion was a real possibility. At the halfway
stage, they were top of the League One table,
and Dele had noticed a huge difference in his
hometown. Suddenly, there were lots of people
walking around, wearing their MK shirts with
pride. It was amazing! If Dele could just help
his local club to reach the Championship, then
that would be the perfect way to say thanks and
goodbye, after eight amazing years.

'No problem,' Pochettino told him. 'You go finish
what you started, and we'll see you back here next
season.'

Agreed! On Deadline Day, 2 February 2015, Dele
signed for Spurs for a fee of £5 million.

'It's a massive club and I'm really happy to be here,' he said to the journalists after posing for lots of photos wearing his new club's white shirt. 'I can't wait to play at White Hart Lane.'

It was a deal that suited everyone: Tottenham, Dele, and, of course MK Dons.

'We are immensely proud of Dele,' Karl Robinson told the media, 'and we are delighted to keep him with us for the rest of the season. Hopefully, we can share some more amazing moments, before he moves on.'

CHAPTER 13

LEAVING LEAGUE ONE ON A HIGH

So, could Dele help lead MK Dons back up to the Championship where they belonged? That was the aim, but it wouldn't be easy. With sixteen games to go in the League One season, they had dropped down to third in the table, behind Bristol City and Swindon Town. And with every game that MK failed to win, Preston North End and Sheffield United were creeping up behind them.

'We can't let this slip now!' Robinson told his players. They had to find their best form again, before their promotion dream faded away.

Colchester United sat second from bottom in

League One, but they were still making life difficult for MK Dons on a tense Tuesday night.

'Come on Dele, we need a moment of magic!' the fans urged as half-time approached.

'I'm trying!' he muttered to himself, growing more and more frustrated. It wasn't the kind of game where he could really show off his silky skills. The ball was in the air most of the time, hoofed from one end to the other. But suddenly after three high headers in a row, Antony Kay booted the ball over the top of the Colchester defence...

Dele was onto it in a flash, before the centre-backs could even react. The ball bounced up perfectly in front of him, asking to be blasted into the roof of the net. But what if he got it wrong? In the end, Dele didn't smash his shot past the keeper; no, he calmly passed it into the bottom corner instead. *1–0!*

Goooooooooooooooooooaaaaaaaaaaaaaaaaalllllllllllll llllllllllllll!!!!!!!!!!!!!!!!!!

'Yes, Dele!' Carl Baker screamed, jumping on his back.

'What a hero!' cheered Dean, their captain.

That goal turned out to be the matchwinner, but it wasn't all good news for MK Dons. Midway through the second half, Dele felt a sudden pain in his ankle. 'Arghhhh!' He winced as he fell to the floor. Was it a bad injury? It was hard to tell at first. He tried his best to run it off, but the pain was getting worse. Eventually, he had no choice but to hobble off the field and down the tunnel to see the physio.

Robinson crossed his fingers and hoped that it was only a minor knock. Sadly, however, it was a lot more serious than that. MK Dons would be without their main man for over a month, right when they needed him most.

'Six whole weeks?' Dele groaned in disbelief. It was his first proper injury, and that long without football sounded like a lifetime. But thanks to his own hard work and the help of the Tottenham doctors, Dele returned in time for the final eight games.

'I'm back!' he cheered as he entered the dressing room.

There was now a big gap at the top of the League One table between Bristol City and everyone else.

Preston were leading the pack, but there was still plenty of time left to catch them. If the Dons finished second, they would be promoted as well, but if they finished third or fourth, they would be thrown into the tricky play-offs instead.

'We've got to grab that second spot,' Dele said with real determination. 'Let's do this!'

Eighteen from the last twenty-four points – that might be enough to get MK back into the Championship. But they weren't taking any chances, and with Dele back, they went eight games unbeaten, picking up twenty-two points along the way!

Swindon Town 0 MK Dons 3,

MK Dons 2 Scunthorpe United 0,

Port Vale 0 MK Dons 0,

Fleetwood Town 0 MK Dons 3…

In the latter game, Dele set up the first with a cross to Lewis Baker, and then scored the third himself, with a right-foot rocket from the edge of the area.

Goooooooooooooooooooaaaaaaaaaaaaaaaaallllllllllll llllllllllll!!!!!!!!!!!!!!!!!!

Meanwhile their rivals Preston could only draw with Gillingham, which meant the gap was now just three points.

'Come on!' Dele roared with pride and passion. They were too good not to go up.

MK Dons 6 Leyton Orient 1

With a drop of the shoulder, Dele fooled the first defender, before curling a beautiful shot in off the post.

Goooooooooooooooooooaaaaaaaaaaaaaaaalllllllllllll llllllllllllllll!!!!!!!!!!!!!!!!!!!!!

Dele's sixteenth goal of the season – Dele made everything look so easy!

MK Dons 3 Doncaster Rovers 0

For once, Dele didn't score himself, but he did set up two goals for Carl instead.

'Cheers, mate!' the striker said, giving him a happy high five.

And there was more good news to follow. Preston had drawn at Port Vale – MK were now only one point behind!

Rochdale 2 MK Dons 3

This was their toughest test, but Dele set up the

winner with a through-ball to Daniel. Yes! The Dons were so close now. It all came down to the final day of the season. They had to win at home against Yeovil Town, and hoped that Preston wouldn't win, away at Colchester.

'We're going up!' Dele declared confidently before kick-off. 'I just know it!'

At half-time, it was so far so good for MK. They were already 4–0 up, whereas Preston were still drawing 0–0. If the scores stayed the same, the Dons would jump up into that precious second spot. However, if Preston scored...

'Come on, Colchester!' Dean shouted across the dressing room.

Dean made it 5–1 to MK in the seventy-fourth minute, but the biggest cheer of the day came eight minutes later. Colchester had taken the lead against Preston! The news soon spread around the stadium.

'Get in!' the MK subs shouted, jumping up and down on the sidelines. That sent a clear message to their teammates on the field.

Would Preston produce an incredible comeback at

Colchester? No, the Dons had done it – they were
going up! When the final whistle blew at Stadium
MK, there were scenes of total chaos. The supporters
stormed the pitch, rushing over to celebrate with
their heroes.

'We're the Dons, we're the Dons, we're the
Dons…'

'We love you, Dele – please don't leave!'

'WE ARE GOING UP, SAY WE ARE GOING UP!'

'Championship, here we come!'

Dele was so happy for the fans, for the coaches
and for his teammates too – they all deserved to
share this moment of glory together. It was a dream
come true to help lead his local team to promotion.

What a season, and what a way to say goodbye!
Dele had delivered big time: sixteen goals, nine
assists and thirty-nine awesome performances at the
age of just eighteen. Unbelievable! Now, it was time
for the new Football League Young Player of the Year
to tackle his next challenge – the Premier League.

CHAPTER 14

PREMIER LEAGUE? NO PROBLEM!

Although Dele felt as self-confident as ever, he tried to be realistic about his targets for his first season at Spurs. As much as he wanted to walk straight into Pochettino's starting line-up, he knew that he would have to take things one step at a time. As he looked around the Tottenham training ground, he was surrounded by top-class internationals now:

Harry Kane and Kyle Walker both played for England,

Hugo Lloris was the keeper and captain of France,

Christian Eriksen was Denmark's danger man,

New signing Son Heung-min was the star of South Korea,

Érik Lamela played alongside Lionel Messi for Argentina,

And then there were the boys from Belgium: Jan Vertonghen and Toby Alderweireld in defence, plus Mousa Dembélé and Nacer Chadli in midfield.

That was a lot of talent in one team! And as Dele soon found out, they lived up to their reputation. At first, every session was a school day, with so much for him to watch and learn:

Harry's finishing,

Christian's creative passing,

Mousa's powerful dribbling,

Érik's tricks,

Son's speed...

Dele was the new kid, and he was hanging out with the big boys now. Was he really ready to fight for a starting spot? Yes, he believed in himself, but he would have to be patient and make the most of the opportunities that came along. Ten starts – that was Dele's aim ahead of his first Spurs season. It didn't take long for him to exceed those expectations...

During the summer of 2015, Dele and his
Tottenham teammates travelled to the USA to take
on the MLS All Stars. After that, they journeyed
to Germany for the Audi Cup, one of the most
prestigious preseason tournaments. Their three
opponents that year?

Real Madrid,

AC Milan,

And Bayern Munich.

'Welcome to the big time!' Eric Dier laughed.
Tottenham were playing against a Real Madrid
team featuring such names as Sergio Ramos, James
Rodríguez, and former Spurs duo Luka Modrić and
Gareth Bale.

'Bring it on!' Dele replied with a big grin. It was
no big deal. If he could do it against Manchester
United, then he could do it against anyone. And
although he was still young, he had already played
nearly one hundred first-team games, so he knew
what he was doing.

Dele made a calm and confident start against
the mighty Real Madrid. He kept calling for the

ball and then playing quick, accurate passes to his left and right.

'That's it, mate,' Mousa, his midfield partner, encouraged him. 'You're a natural!'

In the twenty-third minute, Dele got the ball near the halfway line. In his first months at Tottenham, he had already learnt one very important thing – you got a lot less time on the ball at the top level. His first touch had to be perfect, and he had to think one step ahead, otherwise an opponent would rush in and take the ball away...

This time, the opponent was Modrić. Out of the corner of his eye, Dele could see the little Croatian sprinting towards him to make the tackle. No problem! Dele fooled him with his favourite trick. He waited until the last second and then slid the ball straight through Modrić's legs.

Nutmeg!

Wow, that was a very brave move to attempt against one of the best midfielders in the world! But Dele was determined to show that he was fearless on the football pitch. Modrić had the last laugh, however, as Real Madrid won the match 2–0.

That was only preseason, though. Soon, it was time for the main event to start – the Premier League. And who did Spurs face on the opening day of the 2015–16 season? Dele's old friends, Manchester United.

'Oh good, I've played against them before,' he told Eric. 'And we battered them!'

Although Dele started on the bench at Old Trafford, he did eventually come on for the last fifteen minutes.

Substitution for Tottenham. Replacing Number 15 Eric Dier, Number 20 Dele Alli...

This was it – Dele's Premier League debut! He was determined to succeed, determined to make a difference straight away. However, as hard as he fought for his new club, he couldn't change the score line:

Manchester United 1 Tottenham 0

It wasn't the dream Premier League debut that Dele had been hoping for, but two weeks later, Pochettino gave him another chance, away at

Leicester City. And this time, he had a whole thirty minutes to create some magic.

'Let's do this!' Dele told himself with a focused look on his face.

For the next half an hour, he ran and ran, from box to box, just like Pochettino wanted him to. One minute, Dele was helping out in defence, and the next, he was racing forward to help Harry up front.

'Yes!' he called out as he sprinted into space on the right.

Harry passed left to Nacer instead, but Dele kept running, into the Leicester penalty area.

'Yes!' he called out again, now unmarked at the back post.

Nacer's cross flew just over Harry's head, but there was Dele to flick it bravely past the keeper with a diving header. He nearly crashed into the post along the way, but he didn't care about that. He had scored, and that was all that mattered in the moment. *1–0!*

Goooooooooooooooooooooaaaaaaaaaaaaaaaaalllllllllllll llllllllllllll!!!!!!!!!!!!!!!!!!!!

Even Kasper Schmeichel sitting on him couldn't stop the smile from spreading across Dele's face. What a feeling, and what a time to get off the mark! As he jumped back up, Harry tried to hug him, but Dele dashed away towards the corner to celebrate with all the Tottenham fans. Premier League? No problem! This was where he belonged. Dele had only played thirty minutes of football in England's top division and he had already scored his first goal.

'Get in!' he screamed, punching the air with passion.

Would he be Tottenham's matchwinner? Unfortunately not, because less than two minutes later, Leicester equalised. The match finished 1–1, but from that day onwards, Dele became a starter for Spurs.

CHAPTER 15

ENGLAND'S EXCITING NEW STAR

'Dele for England!'

Now that he was proving himself in the Premier League, people started talking about that next big step – to senior international football.

Although there had been a bit of interest from Nigeria, the country where his dad was from, Dele had always dreamed of wearing the Three Lions for England. England was where he was born and where he was living, and he was a huge fan of the national team, especially when it came to World Cups and Euros.

Plus, Dele had been rising up through the England ranks for years – the Under-17s in 2012, then the

Under-18s in 2014, quickly followed by the Under-19s, where he starred on his debut against Germany. That day, Dele had been the only League One player in a squad full of Premier League talent:

Chelsea's Ruben Loftus-Cheek,

Manchester City's Angus Gunn,

Leicester City's Ben Chilwell,

Tottenham's Harry Winks…

But when did Dele ever let that stop him? Never! It only made him more determined to do well. In the thirty-fifth minute, he robbed the ball off Mahmoud Dahoud in midfield and poked a perfect pass through to England's striker, Bradley Fewster. *1–0!*

Dele wouldn't stay in the Under-19s for long, though. A year later, Gareth Southgate had called him up to the England Under-21s. And now, just one month after that and making his Premier League debut, he was on the move again…

…up into the senior squad!

It seemed so sudden, but actually the England manager, Roy Hodgson, had been scouting Dele for years. His assistant, Ray Lewington, often went to watch MK Dons matches because his son, Dean, was the team's captain. And that's where he had first come across a sixteen-year-old wonderkid who had everything – strength, power, skill, intelligence *and* desire.

'Dele Alli,' Lewington told Hodgson straight away. 'Remember that name because the boy's going to be big!'

Hodgson kept a close eye on Dele's development at MK Dons and then his early days at Tottenham. 'Yes,' the England manager decided, 'he's ready!'

So for the final Euro 2016 qualifiers against Estonia and Lithuania, there were two new call-ups to the England squad:

Liverpool's Danny Ings…

…And Tottenham's Dele Alli!

Wow, what a proud moment – it was hard to believe that this was really happening to him. Just one year earlier, Dele had been battling for League One promotion, and now, he could call legends like Wayne Rooney, James Milner and Gary Cahill his 'teammates'. It was unreal.

'Congratulations!' messaged Harry Kane, who would be there with him for his special night at Wembley.

For most of the match, Dele sat there on the bench, watching and waiting. As the game entered the last ten minutes, his chances of coming on didn't look good. England were only 1–0 up and Ross Barkley was running the show in midfield. Did they really need Dele?

'Oh well, maybe I'll make my debut against Lithuania instead,' he began to think.

But all of a sudden, Harry flicked a long ball onto Jamie Vardy, who crossed it to Raheem Sterling. *2–0!*

Phew! On the sidelines, Hodgson punched the air. Now he could calm down and think about that last substitute... After a quick discussion, Lewington turned to the bench.

'Dele, get ready. You're coming on!'

His tracksuit was off in an instant, and Dele was standing on the touchline, raring to go, wearing the same Number 20 shirt that he wore for Tottenham.

Sadly, those last five minutes flew by in a flash. As

Dele chested the ball down near the centre-circle, the final whistle blew. But he didn't stop playing straight away; no, he tried a cheeky chip from the halfway line! The Estonia keeper made the save, but it just showed Dele's confidence. He wasn't afraid to try anything, even at international level.

Three days later, Dele played the last thirty minutes against Lithuania, as England made it ten wins out of ten. And what did he do when he first got the ball?

Nutmeg!

It was fun being out there on the pitch, playing for his country, but by then, the game was already over. And with Ross having another great game, how was he going to win a starting spot in midfield? Euro 2016 was now only nine months away, and Dele was determined to get there. But how? He would just have to make the most of England's friendlies before the big tournament.

Dele was a second-half sub again in the 2–0 defeat to Spain, but four days later at Wembley, he finally got the chance to start, against France. Playing in a three-man midfield with Ross and his Tottenham teammate, Eric, Dele would have to show off his full range of skills – in defence and in attack. He even had the Number 7 shirt, once worn by the great David Beckham.

'This is it,' Dele told himself before kick-off. 'My time to shine!'

When he saw Harry battling for the ball against three French players, Dele rushed to the rescue. With a big, brave sliding tackle, he won it back and flicked it forward to Nathaniel Clyne, who passed it wide to Wayne.

By that time, Dele was back up on his feet and calling for the ball again. 'Yes, Wazza – I'm in space!'

When the pass arrived, Dele dribbled forward, preparing for the shot. Yes, he had Ross to his left and Harry up ahead, but this was *his* moment. He believed in himself, and so from just outside the box, Dele took aim and fired.

BANG! He watched with growing excitement as the ball flew past the France defence, and then arrowed towards the top right corner. Would his

Tottenham teammate, Hugo Lloris, be able to stop it? No!

Goooooooooooooooooooooaaaaaaaaaaaaaaaaaallllllllllll llllllllllllll!!!!!!!!!!!!!!!!!!

What a fantastic strike on his full England debut! With his arms out wide, Dele ran towards the fans, finally sliding the last bit of his run on his knees.

'Yesssss!' he yelled out with that with a huge smile on his face.

Dele wasn't done yet, though. Early in the second half, he won another midfield battle, stealing the ball off Paul Pogba and playing a beautiful through-ball to Raheem. He curled a cross to Wayne at the back post, who volleyed it in. *2–0!*

As Wayne threw his arms up in the air in triumph, Dele was the first to run over for a hug. They were international teammates now. England's experienced captain and England's exciting new star.

'Great work, Wazza!'

'Cheers, Dele – you started it, though. Well done!'

After that dream debut, surely Hodgson had to play Dele now?

CHAPTER 16

LOSING OUT TO LEICESTER

Dele was on fire, for club and country. The more Premier League games he played, the more brilliant he became.

A volley against Aston Villa,

Another one against West Brom,

And an even better one against Everton...

Away at Crystal Palace, Tottenham were drawing 1–1 with ten minutes to go. But only a win would do for Pochettino's team.

'Come on!' he urged his players on.

Dele got his manager's message. He pushed forward, looking for a way to win it. The Palace defence was getting deeper and deeper, so it would need to be something special.

Harry played a long pass to Christian, who nodded it down to Dele. Right what next? He was just outside the box, and as the ball arrived, he could see Mile Jedinak rushing towards him. Dele had to be quick and he had to be clever, just like during the old days at Heelands Courts.

Tap! He controlled it on the volley,

Flick! He lifted the ball over Jedinak's head,

Turn! He swung his body around, so that he was facing the target,

And *Shoot!* He blasted the ball into the bottom corner. *2–1!*

Goooooooooooooooooooooaaaaaaaaaaaaaaaaallllllllllll llllllllllllll!!!!!!!!!!!!!!!!!!!!

Wow, what a wondergoal! The whole of Selhurst Park was stunned – Palace *and* Tottenham, players *and* supporters. Well, everyone except Dele. He knew that he was capable of all kinds of magic.

'Get in, you hero!' Danny Rose screamed, jumping on his teammate's back.

Dele was the matchwinner, and who was there watching in the crowd? Hodgson, the England manager. The timing was perfect!

Just when other teams were falling apart, Tottenham were growing stronger. With an amazing win away at Manchester City, they jumped up from fourth place to second. Suddenly, anything seemed possible for Spurs, even winning the Premier League title!

First, however, they would have to catch the surprise league leaders, Leicester City. With nine games to go, the Foxes were five points clear at the top.

'We're going to have to win them all from now on!' Pochettino warned his players.

Nine wins in a row? That would be a very difficult task, but Dele was determined to do his best to achieve it.

He set up two goals for Harry against Aston Villa. *2–0!*

And then he set up another goal for Harry against Bournemouth. *3–0!*

Leicester's lead, however, was still five points, and it became seven when Tottenham drew at Liverpool. *Nooooo!* Dele's title dreams were fading fast, but he wasn't giving up. Spurs had to keep believing.

He scored their first goal against Manchester United. *3–0!*

And then he scored two more at Stoke City, including yet another volley. *4–0!*

Just days after his twentieth birthday, Dele was up to ten league goals for the season. The team win was the most important thing, however. And when Leicester drew with West Ham, that meant Tottenham were only five points behind again, with four games to go.

'Come on, we can catch them!' their captain Hugo spurred them on. 'The way we're playing this season, we don't deserve to finish second!'

West Brom at home didn't sound too tricky, but they were a well-organised team and they could be really hard to beat. If Tottenham could make an early breakthrough, though...

Harry played a one-two with Dele and then burst into the box. It looked certain to be goal number twenty-five for the striker, but somehow, he hit the post instead.

'Nooooo!' Dele groaned. He had been sure that Harry would score.

That was the start of a disappointing day for Tottenham, and for Dele in particular. Wherever he went on the pitch, West Brom's tough-tackling midfielder Claudio Yacob was right behind him. The Argentinian always tried to win the ball fairly, but he didn't mind fouling his opponent if he had to.

'Ref!' Dele complained, growing more and more frustrated.

Then in the twenty-sixth minute, for the first time in a Tottenham shirt, he really lost his cool. As Yacob chased back to stop him, Dele swung an arm into his stomach and gave him a sneaky kick.

Although the referee didn't see it, the rest of the world watching at home did. Soon, it was all over social media and Dele was in deep trouble. He played on for the rest of the match, but that turned out to be the end of his season. Afterwards, the FA charged him with violent conduct and handed him a three-game ban.

What a disaster! That meant Tottenham would have to take on Chelsea, Southampton and Newcastle without him. And after that bad draw against West Brom, they now needed to win all three.

At first, Dele was angry at Yacob. 'That's not fair – he fouled me first!'

But once he calmed down, he switched his anger to himself. 'How could I have been so stupid? You just can't react like that, no matter what. Man, I really let my team down!'

It was a horrible feeling that Dele would never forget. He apologised to all his Tottenham teammates and to his fans on Twitter:

'Gutted that my season is over. Will learn from this and come back stronger.'

However, he knew that words alone weren't enough. Dele would have to show he was sorry by becoming an even better player next season. Until then, all he could do was support his club from the sidelines.

'Come on, Spurs!'

Tottenham had to beat Chelsea, otherwise Leicester would be crowned Premier League Champions. At half-time, Dele's teammates seemed to be on track.

Érik slipped a pass through to Harry. *1–0!*

Christian slipped a pass through to Son. *2–0!*

'Yes, lads!' Dele shouted. So far so good.

But in the second half, Spurs lost their confidence and let Chelsea back into the game.

Gary Cahill scored from a goalmouth scramble. *2–1!*

'Uh oh,' Dele thought to himself. Suddenly, it didn't look good for Tottenham's title hopes.

With ten minutes to go, Eden Hazard played a one-two with Diego Costa, and then curled a shot into the top corner. *2–2!*

'Nooooooo!' Dele groaned in despair. All that effort all season long, and now Tottenham would have no trophy to show for it.

Dele was still so young, with lots to learn, and there was plenty of time left for him to win the Premier League title. But losing out to Leicester, and finishing second? No, he couldn't let that happen again.

CHAPTER 17

ANOTHER LEARNING EXPERIENCE AT EURO 2016

Fortunately, Dele didn't have long to dwell on his Premier League disappointment. Because in early June, he was off to France to play for England at Euro 2016. Yes, Dele had done it; he had earned a place in Hodgson's squad.

'Come on!' He celebrated with his fellow Tottenham teammates, Harry, Danny, Kyle and Eric. Together, they were going to make their country proud by finally bringing football home.

Was Dele, aged nineteen, really ready to become England's midfield maestro? Yes! He had followed up his fantastic goal against France with another great game against Germany. This time, he didn't score but he helped lead his team to an incredible comeback.

After sixty minutes in Berlin, England had been 2–0 down and facing a bad defeat. Dele didn't give up, though; he couldn't, not if he wanted to go to Euro 2016. So he kept working hard, running from box to box for his team. Once he had won the ball back, *ZOOM!* he raced forward to help Harry in attack. Dele could do it all; he was the complete midfielder.

Harry scored the first, before Jamie Vardy equalised with a beautiful flick finish. And then with seconds to go, Eric won it with a powerful header. *3–2 to England!*

What a win! The team had shown real strength and spirit. Surely, this was the side that should start at the Euros?

'If they are good enough, they are old enough,' the BBC declared, 'and Alli is good enough.'

The England manager agreed. 'It's an exciting, hungry and energetic bunch of players,' Hodgson said as he announced the twenty-three players that he was taking to France. His midfielders would be:

Adam Lallana,

James Milner,

Jack Wilshere,

Jordan Henderson,

Ross,

Eric,

And Dele!

Amazing, although Dele definitely wasn't going to the Euros to just sit on the bench and have a holiday in the sun. No, he was determined to secure his place in England's starting XI. He didn't mind where he played, just as long as he did play.

When it came to England's first Euro 2016 game against Russia, there he was, Number 20, walking out in his white shirt for kick-off.

It wasn't Dele's greatest game for England, but he still showed flashes of his bravery and brilliance. Every time his team attacked, he burst forward from central midfield to support the strikers. At the end of the first half, Dele found himself near the corner flag, surrounded by three Russian defenders, but he used his sublime skills to escape with the ball.

Olé!

When Eric scored a super free kick in the second half, it looked like England were off to an excellent start. But no, in injury time, Vasili Berezutski jumped the highest at the back post and headed home the equaliser. *1–1!*

'Noooo!' Dele groaned as he watched the ball cross the goal line. England deserved a lot more than a draw, but sometimes, football wasn't fair. It was another painful lesson for him to learn.

In their second match against Wales, England were drawing 1–1 again, and the ninety minutes were almost up. Two games, two points – that wasn't good enough. They really needed to win, otherwise it would put a lot of pressure on that final group game against Slovakia…

As Daniel Sturridge slid a pass through to Jamie, Dele made his move, bursting into the box.

'Yes!' he called out and Jamie played it straight away.

Dele's first touch was good but there were three Welsh players blocking his path to goal. Even he couldn't dance his way through that! So instead, he cleverly dragged the ball to his left, just as a defender dived in.

'Hey, penalty!' Dele cried out as he fell to the floor, but the game carried on because his flick had fallen to Daniel. *BANG!... GOAL! 2–1 to England!*

In a flash, Dele was back up on his feet and racing towards the corner flag to celebrate their crucial goal.

'Get in!' he screamed, jumping up on Danny's back as the England supporters in the stadium went wild all around them.

Their Euro 2016 dream was still alive. A 0–0 draw against Slovakia was enough to take England through to the Round of 16. Phew! There, they would face Iceland, one of the surprise teams of the tournament.

'Don't underestimate them!' Hodgson warned his players. 'They're a strong side and this is the knockouts now, so anything can happen.'

For the first few minutes of the match, it looked like the England players had listened carefully to their manager. Daniel curled a dangerous long ball through to Raheem, who dribbled into the penalty area and was fouled by the Iceland keeper. *Penalty!* Wayne stepped up and scored from the spot. *1–0!*

What a start! After taking the lead, however, England switched off straight away.

Kári Árnason flicked on the long throw and Ragnar Sigurdsson slid in to score. *1–1!*

'Who was marking him?' Joe Hart yelled angrily at his defence. 'Wake up – we haven't won yet!'

Dele tried his best to get England back in front, but his swerving strike flew just over the crossbar.

'Oooooooooo!' Dele sighed deeply, putting his hands to his face. He was so close to scoring at Euro 2016.

England were looking exciting in attack, but dreadful in defence. Dele could only watch in horror as Gylfi Sigurdsson flicked it on to Jón Dadi Bödvarsson, who passed it across to Kolbeinn Sigthórsson.

'Close him down!' Dele cried out with every other England fan in the stadium.

But no, the defenders let the Iceland striker take one touch, then another, and then fire a shot that squirmed through Hart's gloves and over the goal line. *2–1!*

For a moment, the England players just stood

there, frozen in shock. What was going on? Although there was still plenty of time left, they just couldn't find a way to fight back.

Wayne's strikes flew wide,

Harry's headers landed safely in the goalkeeper's gloves,

Dele's scuffed shot looped up high over the bar,

And in the very last minute, Chris Smalling completely messed up his header.

Noooooooooo!

It just wasn't meant to be for England. At the final whistle, Dele dropped to his knees in despair. The team had failed big time, letting everyone down. After all those great expectations, it was such an embarrassing way to exit Euro 2016.

At the lowest point in their international careers, all the England players could do was learn from it and come back stronger. As Dele sat there in the six-yard box in Nice, he tried to think positively. He told himself the same thing that he had told himself after Tottenham's Premier League title disappointment:

'We can't let this happen again.'

CHAPTER 18

DELE THE DESTROYER

Dele's Euros experience did knock his confidence for a little while, but not for long. By Premier League Gameweek Four, he was back on the scoresheet for Spurs.

'Yesssss!' Dele cheered, raising his left arm to the fans who loved him and sang his name:

We've got Alli, Dele Alli
I just don't think you understand,
He only cost five mill,
He's better than Özil,
We've got Dele Alli!

Although Alli was still his surname, he now wore 'Dele' on the back of his shirt instead. That's who he was: Dele the Destroyer. He was back to his best, and so were Tottenham, challenging for the league title once again. Although many of the teams around them looked stronger now, Dele wasn't afraid of anyone.

Manchester City had brought in former Barcelona manager, Pep Guardiola, and spent over £140 million on new players. So what? When they came to White Hart Lane, Tottenham beat them 2–0, even without Harry. Late in the first half, Dele burst between the City centre-backs to reach Son's through-ball and then slid a shot past Claudio Bravo.

Goooooooooooooooooooooaaaaaaaaaaaaaaaalllllllllllll lllllllllllllll!!!!!!!!!!!!!!!!!!!!!

'Come on!' Dele screamed, punching the air again and again.

Chelsea had brought in former Juventus manager, Antonio Conte, and spent nearly £120 million on new players. So what? When they came to White Hart Lane, Dele destroyed them. The Blues had stopped them from winning the 2015–16 title, and now he wanted revenge.

So as Christian looked up to cross the ball in, Dele

positioned himself perfectly, inside the box and in between two Chelsea defenders.

BOOM! He jumped up high, putting plenty of power on the header. The ball looped up and over Thibaut Courtois's desperate dive. 1–0!

Goooooooooooooooooooaaaaaaaaaaaaaaaaallllllllllll llllllllllllllll!!!!!!!!!!!!!!!!!!!

Dele was so delighted that he threw himself in amongst the Tottenham fans.

You legend!

We love you!

The yellow card was totally worth it for that amazing feeling.

Then, early in the second half, Dele did it again. This time, Christian's cross was higher and deeper, but the result was the same. *BOOM!*

Goooooooooooooooooooaaaaaaaaaaaaaaaaallllllllllll llllllllllllllll!!!!!!!!!!!!!!!!!!!

Dele saluted all the Spurs supporters on his way to the corner flag. It was celebration time.

'Come onnnnnnnnnnnnnn!'

Even with Harry back as Spurs' main striker, Dele

still couldn't stop scoring. That was his seventh goal in his last four games, and his tenth of the season. He had already equalled his last year's total and January had only just begun! Back in August, he had set himself a target of fifteen goals, but now he needed to aim even higher – twenty goals? Twenty-five?

'Hey, I'm the top-scorer at Tottenham, okay?' Harry joked as they did their special goal celebration handshake together.

'Well, we'll see about that!' Dele replied, giving his most mischievous grin.

Although they were very different characters, Harry and Dele had three important things in common:

1) They always wanted to win,

2) They loved playing PlayStation,

And most important of all,

3) They loved playing football!

Especially together, in the same Tottenham and England teams. They had a special connection and they always seemed to know where each other would be on the pitch. Before every game, Harry and

Dele discussed their opponents and worked out ways to destroy them.

Harry passed to Dele just outside the West Brom box and then carried on his run, calling for the one-two. But how? Dele had two tall defenders right in front of him! As always, however, he found a quick, clever way out of a tricky situation. He scooped the ball just over their heads and as it dropped down, Harry was there to volley it in. *4–0!*

Another awesome assist for Dele and another hat-trick for Harry! Thanks to their deadly duo, Tottenham were back up to second place in the Premier League table, seven points behind the leaders, Chelsea.

'Not this again!' the Spurs supporters thought to themselves. Last season, they had lost out to Leicester; were they going to lose out to Chelsea this time?

Dele did his very best to create a different ending to the story.

He headed Tottenham back into the game against Manchester City. *GOAL!*

And he scored the winner against Everton with a clever flick. *GOAL!*

Then, when Harry had to miss another four games through injury, Dele stepped forward to become Spurs' big game player again. Even at such a young age, his club could rely on him.

He scored the winner against Southampton from the penalty spot. *GOAL!*

And he set up Son to secure the victory against Burnley. *ASSIST!*

Away at Swansea, Spurs found themselves 1–0 down with six minutes to go. Uh oh, even a draw wouldn't do, not if they wanted to catch Chelsea at the top. As always, Dele desperately wanted to win, and so he pulled up his socks and pressed the 'destroy' button.

Christian's shot pinballed its way through the Swansea box, until it reached Dele, who was all alone at the back post. *1–1!*

'Come on!' he urged his teammates as they ran back for the restart. There was still time for another Tottenham goal... or two.

Son raced through and shot past the keeper. *2–1!*

And then in the final seconds, Dele slid a perfect pass through to Christian, who finished things off. *3–1!*

What a comeback, and again it was Dele who had made the difference! With sixteen goals and seven assists in only his second season in the Premier League, he was well on his way to becoming a world-class player.

But what Dele wanted most was to lift the league title. Tottenham kept on winning, and at last, Chelsea were beaten, by Manchester United. The gap was now just four points, with five games to go. And next up for Spurs? The North London derby against Arsenal.

'It's time to show them that we're the best team in this city!' Dele declared confidently before kick-off.

There was a noisy, nervous atmosphere at White Hart Lane as the players walked out onto the pitch. Tottenham absolutely had to win; they couldn't let their bitter rivals ruin their chances of becoming Premier League Champions. No way!

Early in the second half, Dele dribbled into the

Arsenal penalty area, before cutting the ball back to Christian. His shot was blocked by the keeper, but what about the rebound?

Dele reacted first, even faster than the four Arsenal defenders who were much closer to the bouncing ball. He desperately wanted to win, and with a big, brave stretch of his left leg, he kicked it in. *1–0!*

Goooooooooooooooooooaaaaaaaaaaaaaaaaalllllllllllll llllllllllllll!!!!!!!!!!!!!!!!!!

Dele had done it! And three minutes later, Harry made it 2–0. Thanks to their deadly duo, Tottenham were still in the title race.

But sadly, not for much longer. A week later, they suffered a surprise 1–0 defeat at West Ham. And with a 1–0 win at West Brom, Chelsea were crowned Premier League Champions.

For Dele, it was another frustrating 'nearly' season. He finished with twenty-two goals and thirteen assists in all competitions, plus a second PFA Young Player of the Year award in a row. He was making huge progress as a player, but there was still one major thing missing – a team trophy with Tottenham.

CHAPTER 19

BIG GOALS AGAINST THE BEST

1 November 2017, Wembley Stadium

Playing in the Champions League – that was the dream for so many football-mad kids, including Dele. As a boy, he had loved watching the tournament on TV: the glamorous European giants, the competitive clashes and, of course, the amazing anthem. Dele didn't really like classical music, but 'Zadok the Priest' was brilliant! Hearing it brought back so many special memories.

Now, Dele was lucky enough to be living out his dream. He still found it hard to believe. His Tottenham team were about to take on Real Madrid at Wembley in the greatest club competition in the world. And if they won, they would make it through to the Last 16.

Come on you Spurs!

Dele's first year of Champions League football had been a disappointing one. Although he had scored in the last group game against CSKA Moscow, Tottenham had been knocked out and thrown into the Europa League instead. There, things had got even worse, especially for Dele. He was sent off for a reckless, late tackle against Gent, which meant he had to miss the first three Champions League matches of the next season:

Borussia Dortmund at home,

APOEL Nicosia away,

And Real Madrid away.

But at last, Dele was back, and just in time to face Real Madrid at home. 'His best form is coming' – that's what his manager Pochettino had recently said about him. Well, this was the perfect time for Dele to prove it.

Wow, what a match-up it was going to be: Dele,

Harry and Christian versus four-time Ballon d'Or winner Cristiano Ronaldo, Karim Benzema and Isco.

As the anthem played, however, Dele didn't seem nervous at all. No, he stood there calmly stretching his neck and imagining the great goals he was going to score. To make it to the very top, he had to believe in his own ability. He played football without fear, whether he was in the park with his mates or taking on Ronaldo and Real Madrid at Wembley.

Right from the kick-off, Dele raced around the field, battling hard for every ball. This time, there were no cheeky nutmegs on Modrić; he was a more mature player now and winning was all that mattered. Every time he got the ball, Dele carried it forward, looking to link up with Harry.

Harry wasn't Tottenham's only fantastic finisher, though. Dele was a dangerous goal scorer too. As Kieran Trippier crossed from the right, he was the only Spurs forward in the box, with Real Madrid defenders all around him. It looked like an easy catch for the keeper, but Dele wanted to win so badly that he refused to lose the battle. He outmuscled Nacho and managed to poke the ball past Kiko Casilla. *1–0!*

Gooooooooooooooooooooaaaaaaaaaaaaaaaalllllllllllll llllllllllllllll!!!!!!!!!!!!!!!!!!!!

What a way to return to Champions League action, with a goal against Real Madrid! Dele raced over to the Spurs supporters, with Kieran and Harry right behind him.

'Come on!' they roared together.

After that, Dele's confidence was sky-high. He even played another of his scoop passes before half-time, lifting the ball over the top of the Real defence, but Harry's volley flew straight at the keeper.

'Man, you're on fire!' Harry smiled, giving a big thumbs-up.

Even Ronaldo couldn't ruin Dele's night. The Portuguese striker did eventually score, but it was game over by then.

Just as Real Madrid started to dominate the game, Dele got the ball and dribbled at Casemiro. With a drop of his left shoulder, he beat the Brazilian once,

and then when Casemiro came back for a slide
tackle, Dele skipped past him again.

Olé!

He was into the Real Madrid box now, with
just Sergio Ramos in front of him. *BANG!* Dele's
shot deflected off Ramos, giving the goalkeeper no
chance. *2–0!*

*Goooooooooooooooooooooaaaaaaaaaaaaaaaalllllllllllll
llllllllllllll!!!!!!!!!!!!!!!!!!!!!*

Dele was enjoying the best night of his life, in
front of over 80,000 fans at Wembley. He leapt up,
punching the air like a prize-winning boxer. What
a feeling! Tottenham were beating the twelve-time
European Champions and he had scored both of
the goals.

With the confidence surging through his body,
Dele decided to try a cheeky nutmeg on Ramos. He
couldn't help himself, and it worked!

Olé!

The Real Madrid captain didn't know how to
handle such speed and skill. Soon, Dele launched
another counter-attack, strolling past Ramos with

ease. Near the halfway line, he poked the ball forward to Harry, who then passed it through to Christian. *3–0!*

Unbelievable! As Christian slid across the Wembley grass on his knees, Harry and Dele rushed over to join him, followed by the rest of the team. Together, Tottenham were thrashing Real Madrid!

Dele even had a glorious opportunity to complete his hat-trick. With fifteen minutes to go, Kieran delivered another incredible cross from the right, which dropped down right onto Dele's head. He was unmarked in the middle and just six yards out – he had to score, surely? But no, somehow, he glanced it wide.

'Noooooooo!' Dele groaned, covering his face with his hands and then slapping the crossbar in frustration.

So nearly 4–0! That would have been the perfect end to a perfect night. But never mind, Dele kept battling all the way until the final whistle.

'Get in!' he yelled with his last lungful of energy.

What a performance – they were through to the

Last 16! It was hugs and celebration handshakes all round for Tottenham's Champions League heroes. However, there was no question about who their man of the match was: Dele!

He wasn't having his most successful season in the Premier League so far, but on his Champions League comeback, Dele had just scored two big goals against the best team around. Nothing fazed him, not even going head-to-head with Ronaldo. With him, Harry and Christian in attack, Tottenham were capable of achieving anything.

'We don't want to only compete with these top teams,' Dele told the journalists afterwards, the sweat still shining on his calmly focused face. 'We want to be beating them.'

CHAPTER 20

WORLD CUP 2018

Dele had been waiting a long time for the summer of 2018. Why? Because it was a World Cup summer! Growing up, those were some of his happiest memories. Dele loved everything about the tournament: the barbeques, the sense of optimism, the England flags everywhere, and of course, the football itself.

This time, however, he wouldn't be at home, watching on TV with the Hickfords, like in 2010 and 2014. No, he would be out on the pitch, playing for his country!

England announced their 2018 World Cup squad

with a special video, where each player's name was revealed one by one. Raheem was first, then John Stones, then Trent Alexander-Arnold…

Eventually, three excited teenagers appeared on screen, huddled around the centre-circle of an artificial football pitch that was similar to the one at Heelands Courts.

'DELE ALLI,' they cheered, bouncing up and down together. 'OI OI OI!'

Soon, Dele's family and friends were bouncing up and down too.

'Congratulations, we're so proud of you!' cried Alan and Sally.

'Nice one, bro – I knew you could do it,' Harry said, giving him a hug. After his own football career had been ended by injury, he was now Dele's agent as well as his best friend. 'Right, we better pack our bags – Russia, here we come!'

A lot had changed for England since their Euro 2016 disaster. First of all, Roy Hodgson had been replaced as manager by Sam Allardyce and then by Dele's old Under-21 manager, Gareth Southgate.

As a former England international himself, Southgate understood the nation's expectations and he had big plans for the future: 'I'm determined to give the country a team that they're proud of and one that they're going to enjoy watching play and develop.'

Dele liked the sound of that, and he liked working with Southgate. He was building an exciting new England squad and Dele wanted to be a big part of it, starting with the 2018 World Cup.

'It's an honour to be named in the England squad for the World Cup,' he posted on social media alongside two photos: one of him boarding the team plane and the other of him back in his early international days with the Under-17s. 'It's a dream come true! Get me to Russia!!!'

Dele and his teammates were determined to move on from the painful memories of Euro 2016 and give the country something to cheer about.

Ahead of the tournament, Southgate had switched the England formation from a 4-3-3 to a 3-5-2 with attacking wing-backs. It was new

for some, but not for Dele. He had played in
that formation many times at Tottenham, under
Pochettino. With Kieran and Danny flying down the
flanks, Dele's role was to run box-to-box through
the middle, getting back to win the ball and then
forward to help Harry up front. That's how they
had thrashed the mighty Real Madrid, so would it
work for England too?

'Of course, it will!' Dele declared confidently
as the team walked out for their first group game
against Tunisia. Southgate had created a great squad
spirit, where everyone got on well and knew their
roles. With Jordan Henderson sitting deeper in
defensive midfield, Dele and Jesse Lingard had the
freedom to attack as much as possible.

In only the second minute of the match, Dele
raced onto Jordan's long pass and looked to pick
out Raheem in the middle. The Tunisia centre-back
blocked the cross, but Dele got a second go. He
poked it across to Jesse, whose shot was saved by
the keeper.

So close already! Jesse stood there with his hands

to his mouth, and Dele with his hands on his head. What an amazing start that would have been...

'Keep going – the goal is coming!' Harry, their captain, clapped and cheered.

Just seven minutes later, it arrived. The Tunisia keeper managed to stop John's thunderous header, but the rebound fell to Harry, who hardly ever missed. *1–0 to England!*

'Get in!' Dele yelled out as he joined the player pile-on.

England were on top and they soon had chances to make it 2–0. Kieran's cross whistled through the gap between Dele and Harry, and then Jordan's long-range rocket flew straight at the keeper.

The Three Lions were attacking with such style and confidence, but out of the blue, they conceded a penalty. *1–1!* Although the equaliser came as a shock for England, they still had plenty of time left to score a winner...

But Dele's clever flick header was cleared off the line,

Then Jesse hit the post,

And then the referee refused to give a penalty when Harry was clearly fouled.

Uh oh – were England heading for another disappointing draw? Dele ran and ran but with ten minutes to go, he had to come off. He had picked up an injury in the first half, and the pain was getting worse.

Instead, it was Harry who was England's hero yet again. With a swing of his strong neck, he powered the ball into the net. *2–1!*

'Yesssss!' Dele shouted on the sidelines with the rest of the squad. *Phew!* It hadn't been easy, but in the end, England had that first World Cup win that they were looking for.

On to the next game, but would Dele be able to play against Panama? 'Frustrating to have picked up a slight injury on Monday,' he posted on Twitter. 'Will do everything in my power to get back to full fitness asap!'

England didn't need Dele for that game anyway. He watched from the bench as the goals went flying in. *1–0, 2–0, 3–0... 6–1!*

'Man, I would definitely have scored today!' he joked with Harry, who had bagged a hat-trick.

Oh well, Dele's first World Cup goal would just have to wait. After resting for the final group game against Belgium, he came back for England's Round of 16 clash with Colombia.

In a fierce and fiery match, Dele managed to last the first eighty minutes. As he trudged off the field, England were 1–0 up and on their way to the quarter-finals. But deep in injury time, disaster struck. Yerry Mina scored from a corner, and the game went to extra-time and then... PENALTIES!

For Dele, it was so difficult to watch. He wanted to be out there with his teammates on the halfway line, and then stepping up to score for England. Instead, however, he had to watch helplessly from the sidelines.

'Go on!' he muttered as Harry and Marcus Rashford made it two out of two.

'Noooo!' he groaned when Jordan missed.

'Yessss!' he cheered when Mateus Uribe missed too.

After that, it was all good news:

Kieran scored, then Jordan Pickford saved from Carlos Bacca, and then Eric stepped up to score the winner. England were through to the World Cup quarter-finals!

'Come on!' Dele roared as he raced over to join in the joyful celebrations. The pile of players was already pretty high, but he still jumped on the top.

Not only had England won, but they had won A PENALTY SHOOT-OUT! It was the first time that had happened in twenty-two years, and it filled the fans with hope and confidence.

The players, however, were taking it one step at a time. First, they needed to beat Sweden to book their place in the semi-finals.

It was Harry who gave them the lead, but not Harry Kane; no, Harry Maguire, their big centre-back with a head as hard as stone. *BOOM! 1–0!*

For the next twenty minutes, England's lead looked comfortable, but they really didn't want a repeat of the Tunisia game. A second goal would really help to settle things down...

As Jesse curled a cross into the box, Dele made his move at the back post, racing in behind his marker's back. The ball was coming straight towards him; he wouldn't get a better chance than this. How many times had he scored headers like this for Tottenham? Loads! Dele jumped up high, pushing his head towards the ball with power. *BOOM!* It flew past the keeper before he could really react. *2–0!*

Goooooooooooooooooooooaaaaaaaaaaaaaaaaallllllllllll llllllllllllllll!!!!!!!!!!!!!!!!!!!!

Only once the ball had dropped down into the net, did Dele allow himself to celebrate.

'YESSSSSSS!' he exploded with emotion.

Despite his injury problems, Dele had fought his way back into the team and now, he had done it. He had scored his first World Cup goal.

'Wow! World Cup semi-finals,' Dele wrote on social media. 'Let's go, England!'

The next day, the players watched the videos of all the amazing celebrations back home. They had already given their country lots to cheer about in

Russia, but what if they could return with the World Cup trophy? They would be heroes forever!

Once more, Dele dared to dream. There were no nerves or doubts; he prepared like it was just a normal game, rather than a World Cup semi-final. In the England dressing room in Moscow, he went through the same old routine:

Right sock, then right boot (size 10), then right shin pad (the same ones he had worn since he was eleven years old),

Left sock, then left boot (size 10-and-a-half), then left shin pad...

Right, ready!

In the fourth minute against Croatia, Dele collected Jesse's pass and drove forward towards goal, until he was fouled by his old Real Madrid opponent, Modrić. *Free kick to England!* The position was perfect for a curler from Kieran. *1–0!*

'Yes, Tripps, you legend!' Dele cried out as he chased after his Tottenham teammate. England were on their way to the World Cup Final!

It was the perfect start and before half-time,

Harry had two glorious chances to make it 2–0. Unfortunately, he missed them both and as the second half went on, Croatia came back into the game. In the sixty-eighth minute, Šime Vrsaljko's cross flew all the way through to Ivan Perišić. *1–1!*

As the goal went in, Dele's heart sank. After all that running, after all that defending. His energy was gone; he was exhausted. He didn't give up, and England battled on into extra-time, but it was Croatia who grabbed the winning goal and a place in the World Cup Final.

At the final whistle, Dele dropped to the grass. He was absolutely devastated. He had never known a feeling like it – disappointment, rage, regret and pride all rolled into one. It was gutting to get so close to the final. The players had given everything, but it just wasn't quite enough. However, although they hadn't brought the World Cup home, they *had* brought football home. England had fallen in love with its national team once more.

Once he'd had a bit of time to calm down and think, Dele wrote a message to his social media followers:

'I want to thank everyone for the support we've received. This is going to take a while to get over, but I truly believe this team has a bright future and we will make England proud again!'

CHAPTER 21

EUROPEAN EXCITEMENT

'Back to work,' Dele posted on Twitter as he returned to Tottenham for preseason training. After a relaxing holiday, he was now ready to put his World Cup woes behind him and focus on club football again. Dele had a team trophy to try and win.

Second, second, third – for each of the last three years, Spurs had come so close to lifting the Premier League title. They had also reached two FA Cup semi-finals, but sadly, there was still no silverware to show for all their success. And if Spurs didn't win something soon, then their star players – Harry, Christian, Son – might move on to other clubs...

And, of course, Dele, might do the same. At the

age of twenty-two, he had already led a very eventful life, but he was about to set out on his most exciting adventure yet.

It only took Dele eighteen minutes to score his first goal of the 2018–19 season. As Serge Aurier looked up to cross the ball into the Newcastle box, he spotted Dele racing in at the back post, waving his arm frantically. It was a classic team move, but it seemed to work every time.

PING! Serge's cross was perfect, and Dele did the rest. He sprang up to meet the ball and nodded it down into the bottom corner.

Goooooooooooooooooooaaaaaaaaaaaaaaaalllllllllllll llllllllllllll!!!!!!!!!!!!!!!!!!!!

After a quick hug with Harry, he turned to the crowd and raised his right hand to his right eye, flipping it around to make a funny salute.

New season, new celebration, but same old super Dele.

As with most exciting adventures, however, there were also moments of misfortune. Dele hurt his hamstring while playing for England in September and had to miss four Premier League games, plus three crucial European ties:

Inter Milan 2 Tottenham 1,

Tottenham 2 Barcelona 4,

PSV Eindhoven 2 Tottenham 2…

Only one point from three games – uh oh, halfway through the group stage, it looked like Spurs' Champions League campaign was already over.

But when Dele came back, he helped to turn things around for his team.

…Tottenham 2 PSV Eindhoven 1,

Tottenham 1 Inter Milan 0…

With time running out, Moussa Sissoko dribbled the ball forward from midfield, and all the way into the Inter box.

'Yes!' Dele called out for it on the edge of the area.

When the pass arrived, it was slightly behind him. So rather than shoot for goal himself, Dele spun quickly and passed the ball into Christian's path. *1–0!*

'Yessss!' the two Tottenham players yelled at each other.

What an important goal, to keep their Champions League hopes alive! Now, they just needed to win their final group game, and they would be through to the Last 16. The only problem: the team they had to beat was Barcelona... away at the Nou Camp.

That was going to be tough, but Dele was always up for a challenge. He had already helped Tottenham to thrash Ronaldo's Real Madrid, so why not Lionel Messi's Barcelona too? They had to believe.

But even Dele had a few doubts, when Ousmane Dembélé raced through to score after only seven minutes. Oh dear, Tottenham's tough task had just got even tougher.

There was plenty of time left though, and over in Italy, PSV had just taken the lead. *Phew!* If Inter lost too, then Spurs could still go through.

That all changed, however, when Mauro Icardi scored for Inter midway through the second half. Suddenly, they jumped up into second place. So, what could Tottenham do to fight back?

Although Dele wasn't having his greatest game, he never gave up, and neither did his teammates. With five minutes to go, Christian passed it to Érik, who passed it to Harry, who crossed it to Lucas Moura. *1–1!*

'Get in!' Together, Tottenham had grabbed the goal that they needed. But would that be enough? Yes! Over in Italy, Inter could only draw with PSV. Somehow, Spurs had pulled off the impossible – they were through to the Champions League Last 16!

Dele celebrated by helping to destroy Arsenal in the North London derby a week later. Away at the Emirates, he created Tottenham's first goal with a beautiful chipped pass to Son. *1–0!*

Then, early in the second half, Harry played a similar pass to Dele, who was through one-on-one with the Arsenal keeper. Could he score? Of course he could – and he did it in style. With the outside of his right boot, Dele dinked the ball over Petr Čech and into the bottom corner. *2–0!*

Gooooooooooooooooooooaaaaaaaaaaaaaaaallllllllllll llllllllllllll!!!!!!!!!!!!!!!!!!!

Wow, what a finish!

Nothing could ruin Dele's big North London derby, not even being hit on the head by a bottle. At first, Dele turned around angrily to shout up into the stand, but then he changed his mind. That would only make things worse. So instead, he swapped his glare for a mischievous grin raising two fingers on one hand and making a zero with the other: 2–0 – just in case the Arsenal supporters had forgotten what the score was.

It was so far so good for Dele's season, but sadly, by the time the Champions League returned in February, he was injured again. It was another thigh strain and it meant he had to miss both legs of Tottenham's tie with Borussia Dortmund. Fortunately, they won it 4–0 even without him.

'Sorry mate, I don't think we need you anymore,' Harry said afterwards. 'Nah, just joking! You'll be back for the quarter-finals, right?'

'Try stopping me!' Dele replied.

In the Champions League quarter-finals, Spurs were up against their Premier League rivals,

Manchester City, and it would be their first big
European night at their brand-new, 60,000-seater
stadium.

They won 1–0 at the Tottenham Hotspur Stadium,
thanks to a penalty save from Hugo and a great goal
from Son. Now, Spurs just had to stay strong at the
Etihad.

'Bring it on!' cheered Dele, but it turned out to be
the craziest football match he had ever played in.

First, Raheem curled a shot into the bottom corner.
1–1 on aggregate!

Then Dele's through-ball to Christian was cut out,
but the rebound fell to Son. *2–1 to Spurs!*

Then Christian passed to Son, who scored again.
3–1!

Then Bernardo Silva's shot deflected in off Danny.
3–2!

And finally, Raheem raced in at the back post to
make it 3–3!

Five goals in only twenty-one minutes – what on
earth was going on? Things did calm down after that.
A whole thirty-eight minutes passed before the next

goal, although unfortunately, it was Sergio Agüero who got it. *4–3 to City!*

Could Tottenham come back again? Yes, and in the strangest way! Kieran's corner-kick bounced off Fernando Llorente's hip and into the City net. After a quick VAR check, the goal was given: *4–4!*

'Come on!' the Tottenham players cheered, standing together in front of their fans.

As if that wasn't enough European excitement for one night, there was still one more twist in the tale. In injury time, Bernardo Silva intercepted Christian's pass and flicked it forward to Agüero, who squared it to Raheem, who fired a shot past Hugo. *5–4 to City!*

'Noooooo!' Dele growled as he watched from near the halfway line. Not another devastating defeat...

But wait! VAR was checking the goal again. And after what felt like hours of agony for Dele, the referee finally made his decision:

Agüero was offside – no goal!

Unbelievable scenes! Now, if Tottenham could just hold on for three more minutes, they would go through on away goals. It felt like forever, but they held on – and they were through.

'Yes, yes, yes!' Dele screamed, as he raced around the pitch hugging and high fiving everyone he saw. It felt too good to be true.

The Tottenham team formed a line and took a bow in front of their supporters, but it was only later that their incredible achievement really sank in. Somehow, despite all the drama along the way, Spurs were still in the Champions League, and Dele wanted the whole world to know it:

'UNREAL NIGHT!! WE'RE IN THE SEMIS!!'

CHAPTER 22

CHAMPIONS LEAGUE HIGHS AND LOWS

For the first leg of their Champions League semi-final against Ajax, the Tottenham team were without four of their star players:

The two Harrys – Kane and Winks,

Érik,

And Son.

Wow, they were missing a lot of goals and creativity in attack! Oh well, Spurs would just have to rely on their strong team spirit and their stars who were available:

Christian,

Lucas,

Hugo,

And, of course, Dele. With the pressure on, could he step up and become Tottenham's big game player once again?

Not in the first leg at the new White Hart Lane, unfortunately. As the teams walked out onto the pitch, Dele looked at the inspiring sight to his right. The Tottenham fans had formed a wall of white and blue, displaying the words, 'DARE TO DO'. That was their message to the players, but sadly even a deafening euphoric home crowd couldn't save Spurs from a disappointing defeat.

In the fifteenth minute, Hakim Ziyech slipped a perfect pass through to Donny van de Beek. *1–0 to Ajax!*

And that's how it stayed, despite Dele's best efforts. His first shot from the edge of the area was blocked by a defender and then he fired a volley straight at the Ajax keeper.

'Arggh!' Dele snarled, kicking the air in frustration. Harry would have scored it and he knew it.

Early in the second half, the scene looked set for a Kieran-to-Dele classic. But as the ball looped towards him at the back post, Dele couldn't jump high enough to head it down.

'Nooooooo!'

A 1–0 home defeat – it didn't look good, but it wasn't a total disaster for Tottenham. Dele still believed; they had battled back before to make it out of Group B and then past Manchester City. Their best chance of winning the Champions League wasn't over yet.

Son and Érik were back for the second leg in Amsterdam, but Spurs were still without the two Harrys. Calm and focus would be key, plus goals, of course. Dele knew that he would have to do better this time, especially in attack. He had to make the difference.

'Come on, we can do this!'

By half-time, however, it really did look like game over. Ajax were 2–0 up on the night, and 3–0 up on aggregate. To make it to the Champions League Final, Tottenham would have to score three now.

'The next goal is going to be crucial,' Pochettino

told his players in the dressing room. 'If we score it, it's game on!'

Challenge accepted! Dele never even thought about giving up. Instead, he clenched his fists with determination. Tottenham had come too far in the tournament to get knocked out without a fight. Dele was desperate to win his first team trophy at the club, and this was their last chance of the season. There were forty-five minutes left and they had to give it everything.

Early in the second half, Danny played a long pass up to Lucas, who flicked it on to Dele as he entered the Ajax half. As he dribbled towards the penalty area, Dele twisted and turned his way past Frenkie de Jong, before threading a beautiful pass through to Lucas. *3–1!*

Tottenham had scored the next goal – it was game on! As Dele ran back for the restart, he could feel the belief returning all around him. They could do this; they could pull off their most incredible comeback ever. They just needed two more goals now...

Spurs were on the attack, with their confidence back. Kieran delivered a dangerous cross to Fernando, who looked certain to score from three yards out. Somehow, however, the Ajax keeper saved it.

Nooooo, what a wasted opportunity!

But wait! The ball spilled out to Lucas, who weaved his way through the crowded box, turned and curled an unstoppable left-foot strike into the bottom corner. *3–2!*

Woah, Tottenham now only needed one more goal to win it. Was it going to be their night, after all?

'Go on!' Pochettino urged his team forward.

The last fifteen minutes were full of end-to-end drama.

Ziyech hit the post for Ajax,

Then Jan headed the ball against the bar.

Was that it – Tottenham's last chance? No, in the final seconds of injury time, Fernando knocked a long ball down to Dele, on the edge of the 'D'. There was no time to think; it was all about instinct now.

Dele had spotted a bit of space in between the Ajax defence, and so with a quick swivel of his body and a delicate flick of his right foot, he placed the pass right there…

ZOOM! Lucas was onto it, beating Matthijs de Ligt to the ball…

'Finish it, finish it!' Dele muttered as he watched.

…And with another swing of his left foot, Lucas found the bottom corner with the last kick of the game. *3–3!*

Their incredible comeback was complete! As the Ajax players collapsed to the grass, the Tottenham team went wild. Against all the odds, they had done it – they were into the Champions League Final!

It all felt like a dream to Dele. Had that really just happened? Yes, it had, and he had helped make a difference! Lucas was Tottenham's hat-trick hero, but it was Dele's quick thinking that had created his winning goal.

The celebrations went on and on, moving from the pitch to the dressing room, where the music played, and the champagne sprayed. None of the Tottenham players wanted their magical moment to end. It was hard to describe the feeling, but Dele did his best:

'BEST NIGHT OF MY LIFE!! MADRID HERE WE COME!!'

However, after that Champions League high came a Champions League low. After only two minutes of the final in Madrid, Tottenham were losing 1–0 to Liverpool.

Sadio Mané burst into the box and his pass bounced off Moussa's arm. *Penalty!*

'No way!' Dele thought, stopping still on the edge of the area. He couldn't watch as Mohamed Salah scored from the spot.

It was the worst possible start for Tottenham, and this time, they couldn't turn things around. As hard as he tried, Dele couldn't get into the game. His touch was heavy, and he was missing easy tackles. What was going on? He was meant to be a big game player, and this was the biggest game of all!

When Dele did finally get a chance to shoot, he chipped the ball so high that Alisson had an easy catch to make.

'Ohhhh!' Dele sighed as his shoulders slumped. Although it wasn't an easy chance, he still expected better of himself. So, what else could he do to make a difference for his team? He had to keep trying.

Dele played a slick pass to Son to set up a quick counter-attack, but Virgil van Dijk was there to deal with the danger.

Dele burst in at the back post to meet Kieran's cross, but the ball was a little too high, and so was his header.

Dele set up Son again, but Alisson dived down to save his shot.

No, this time it just wasn't to be for Tottenham. And in the eighty-first minute, Dele's night came to an early end. When he saw his number, '20', flash up on the electronic subs board, he couldn't believe it. What?! Why was Pochettino taking him off, just when he was getting into the game? As he stormed off the field, Dele was so furious that he threw his drinks bottle against the back of the dug-out. *THUD!*

While Dele sat there sulking on the bench, Divock Origi made it 2–0 to Liverpool. Game over, and Tottenham's dream of winning the Champions League trophy over.

Dele did go up to collect his runners-up medal, but he wasn't going to wear it proudly around his neck. That would have to wait, until he eventually won the competition.

'I'm heartbroken,' Dele admitted honestly in the press conference afterwards. 'It's been an amazing journey for us as a team, but now, we need to take this painful feeling and use it to drive us on next season.'

CHAPTER 23

NEW MOTIVATION FROM MOURINHO

During his summer break of 2019, Dele thought long and hard about that painful loss to Liverpool, and about his future too. Although he was proud to be part of such a successful Tottenham team, he couldn't help feeling a bit frustrated. Were they ever going to win something? Semi-finalists in the FA Cup *and* the League Cup; runners-up in the Premier League (twice) *and* the Champions League. Each year, they worked so hard to get so close to a trophy.

Dele tried his best to ignore the comments on social media, but he knew what people were saying:

'They'll never win anything – that's Spurs for you!'

'Kane, Alli, Pochettino – they're good but you

can't call them great. I mean, where are their trophies?'

It was now or never for Spurs as the 2019–20 season kicked off. They couldn't keep finishing second forever, especially not now that they had strengthened the squad by spending £80 million on French midfielder Tanguy Ndombele and young English winger Ryan Sessegnon.

But after eight Premier League matches, Tottenham found themselves way down in ninth position, and Dele had only played a total of thirty minutes. For the first few games, he had been injured, but once he got fit again, Pochettino left him on the bench.

'What's going on?' he wondered as Spurs lost 3–0 to Brighton without him. 'What did I do wrong?'

Their results were even worse in the Champions League. After a 2–2 draw with Olympiakos, Bayern Munich thrashed them 7–2 at the Tottenham Hotspur Stadium. How humiliating! Just four months after reaching the Champions League Final, they were falling apart.

Something had to change and that something turned

out to be the manager. After five league games without a win, Daniel Levy decided to sack Pochettino.

Dele couldn't believe it; after everything they'd been through together! 'I can't thank this man enough,' he posted on Twitter. 'He's taught me so much and I'm so grateful for everything he's done for me.'

Now, though, it was time for a fresh start. The next day, Spurs announced the new man in charge: José Mourinho.

The Portuguese manager wasn't the most popular choice, but he certainly had a record for winning. He had won three Premier league titles with Chelsea, plus two Champions League trophies with Porto and Inter Milan. And he was famous for getting the best out of his players, including one of Dele's childhood heroes: Frank Lampard.

Growing up, Dele wanted to be just like Lampard and Gerrard – box-to-box midfielders who scored lots of goals and played with such drive and determination. So, maybe Mourinho could help him to find his best form again...

'Are you Dele Alli or are you his brother?' his
new manager asked him at one of their first training
sessions together.

What?! What was this guy talking about?

'I'm Dele,' he replied. 'Obviously.'

'Okay, good – then I need you to play like Dele,'
his manager told him, 'like you did in your first two
seasons at Tottenham.'

Mourinho wanted Dele to go back to doing what he
did best – attacking. For the last few years, Pochettino
had played him in a slightly deeper midfield role,
but now he was being asked to become a Number
10 again. Goals and assists – that's what his team
needed from him. So, with that extra motivation from
Mourinho, Dele set out to rediscover his best form.

Against West Ham, he set up the first goal for Son,
with a simple turn and pass. *1–0!*

Then, after slipping over, he skilfully managed to
flick another pass through to Son, while he was still
down on the floor.

Olé!

Dele's quick, clever thinking had returned. Son

raced down the wing and crossed it into Lucas. *2–0!*

'That was the real Dele,' Mourinho declared happily after his first match as manager.

That strong start didn't last long, however. Three days later in the Champions League, Tottenham went 2–0 down at home against Olympiakos. If they lost, they might not make it through the group stage. But just before half-time, a determined Dele helped lead another incredible Spurs comeback.

As the Olympiakos centre-back went to clear away Serge's cross, he completely missed his kick! The ball whistled through the six-yard box until it reached Dele, who had snuck in between two defenders, like he always loved to do. *2–1!*

Goooooooooooooooooooooaaaaaaaaaaaaaaaalllllllllllll llllllllllllll!!!!!!!!!!!!!!!!!

'Come on!' Dele urged his teammates. 'It's not over yet!'

From a quick throw-in, Lucas set up Harry. *2–2!*

Dele tricked his way into the box and then crossed the ball into the danger zone. Son got the flick-on and Serge finished it off beautifully. *3–2!*

And Dele wasn't done yet. A minute later, he dribbled the ball all the way down the left wing, from deep inside his own half. He tried to shrug off the Olympiakos defender, but he fouled him eventually. *Free kick!* Christian curled it in, and Harry headed it home. *4–2!*

'Champions League Last 16, here we come!' Tottenham's attacking trio celebrated together.

In his first two games under Mourinho, Dele had won two man of the match awards, and the key moments kept on coming. Against Bournemouth, Dele made two of his trademark runs, on both occasions bursting into the box and finding the net:

Goooooooooooooooooooaaaaaaaaaaaaaaaalllllllllllll llllllllllllllll!!!!!!!!!!!!!!!!!!!!

Goooooooooooooooooooaaaaaaaaaaaaaaaalllllllllllll llllllllllllllll!!!!!!!!!!!!!!!!!!!!

'Get in!' he roared, punching the air with passion. The old Dele was definitely back, and so was his big smile.

At the age of twenty-four, he had already achieved so much in his career, but he was always hungry for more. More goals, more assists and more glory. When he made the big move to Tottenham from his boyhood club, MK Dons, he had shown no fear, and with help from Harry and Pochettino, he had proved himself in the Premier League straight away.

From there, Dele's talent and determination had taken him all the way to the 2018 World Cup with England, and the 2019 Champions League Final with Spurs. Although both tournaments had ended in disappointment, Dele wasn't giving up. No way – that wasn't his style. Dele saw every setback as a lesson to be learned, with every step taking him closer to becoming a world-class winner.

DELE ALLI
HONOURS

MK Dons
🏆 Football League One runner-up: 2014–15

Tottenham
🏆 UEFA Champions League runner-up: 2018–19

Individual
🏆 Football League Young Player of the Year: 2014–15
🏆 Milton Keynes Dons Players' Player of the Year: 2014–15
🏆 BBC Goal of the Season: 2015–16
🏆 PFA Young Player of the Year: 2015–16, 2016–17

DELE ALLI

20 **THE FACTS**

NAME: Bamidele Jermaine Alli

DATE OF BIRTH: 11 April 1996

AGE: 24

PLACE OF BIRTH: Milton Keynes

NATIONALITY: England

BEST FRIEND: Harry Hickford

CURRENT CLUB: Tottenham

POSITION: CAM

THE STATS

Height (cm):	188
Club appearances:	307
Club goals:	86
Club trophies:	1
International appearances:	37
International goals:	3
International trophies:	0
Ballon d'Ors:	0

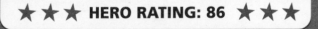

★ ★ ★ **HERO RATING: 86** ★ ★ ★

GREATEST MOMENTS

26 AUGUST 2014,
MK DONS 4–0 MANCHESTER UNITED

Dele had already made a name for himself in League
One, but this was the night he proved himself against
Premier League opponents. Although he didn't
score or set up any of the goals, Dele outplayed the
whole Manchester United midfield, at the age of
only eighteen. It was a classy cup performance that
really impressed Mauricio Pochettino, the Tottenham
manager.

3 MAY 2015,
MK DONS 5–1 YEOVIL TOWN

After signing for Spurs, Dele went straight back to
MK Dons on loan. He was determined to get his
hometown club promoted and this was the day he
did it. Dele didn't score or set up any goals, but
he dominated in midfield. Plus, he had already
contributed sixteen goals and nine assists that season.
This was the perfect way to say goodbye to the Dons.

1 NOVEMBER 2017,
TOTTENHAM 3–1 REAL MADRID

Dele already had a reputation as a big game player,
and he confirmed it here against Cristiano Ronaldo's
Real Madrid in the Champions League at Wembley.
He slid in bravely to score the first goal, used his skills
to score the second, and then helped set up the third
for Christian Eriksen. To cap off a perfect performance,
Dele even gave Sergio Ramos the nutmeg treatment!

7 JULY 2018,
SWEDEN 0–2 ENGLAND

Up until this point, it had been a frustrating first World Cup for Dele. He had to miss England's last two group games because of injury. Although he returned against Colombia, this was the game when Dele announced he was really back. With England 1–0 up, he made his classic back-post run to head home Jesse Lingard's cross and secure their place in the semi-finals.

8 MAY 2019,
AJAX 2–3 TOTTENHAM

On this miraculous night, Tottenham pulled off an incredible Champions League comeback to make it through to the final. At half-time, 2–0 down, it looked all over for Spurs, but Dele didn't give up. He started the fightback by setting up the first goal for Lucas Moura and he finished it by doing the same again. With the last kicks of the game, Dele flicked a clever pass through to Lucas, who fired in the winner and completed a hat-trick.

PLAY LIKE YOUR HEROES

BURST INTO THE BOX LIKE DELE ALLI

STEP 1: Battle bravely for the ball in the middle of the pitch, using all your strength and determination.

STEP 2: Once your team have it back, go go go!

STEP 3: When the ball goes out wide, start making your move towards the back-post area. Take your time, though – you want to catch your opponents by surprise!

STEP 4: As the cross comes in, make your big burst into the box, in between two defenders.

STEP 5: If the ball's coming in low, stretch out your leg and slide in if you have to. *BANG!*

STEP 6: If the ball's coming in high, watch it carefully all the way and time your jump. *BOOM!*

STEP 7: *GOAL!* With a mischievous grin on your face, celebrate in a cool way that the kids will want to copy.

TEST YOUR KNOWLEDGE

QUESTIONS

1. Who was Dele's first football hero?

2. What were the MK Dons called up until 2004?

3. How old was Dele when he moved in permanently with the Hickfords?

4. Who predicted that Dele was 'going to be a superstar'?

5. Dele scored on his senior MK Dons debut – true or false?

6. Name at least three members of the Manchester United team that Dele's MK Dons thrashed 4–0 in 2014.

7. How much did Tottenham pay to sign Dele in 2015?

8. Which manager handed Dele his England debut?

9. Tottenham finished second in the Premier League for two years in a row – 2015–16 and 2016–17. Which teams won those titles?

10. Who set up Dele's goal against Sweden at the 2018 World Cup?

11. Dele set up two goals in Tottenham's 2019 Champions League semi-final against Ajax but which of his teammates scored a hat-trick?

Answers below. . . No cheating!

1. *Steven Gerrard* 2. *Wimbledon* 3. *Thirteen* 4. *MK Dons manager Karl Robinson* 5. *False – but he did score a screamer in his second appearance!* 6. *Any of the following: David de Gea, Johnny Evans, Michael Keane, Nick Powell, Anderson, Shinji Kagawa, Danny Welbeck, Chicharito* 7. *£5 million* 8. *Roy Hodgson* 9. *Leicester City and Chelsea* 10. *Jesse Lingard* 11. *Lucas Moura*

CAN'T GET ENOUGH OF
Ultimate Football Heroes?

**Check out heroesfootball.com
for quizzes, games, and competitions!**

**Plus join the Ultimate Football Heroes
Fan Club to score exclusive content
and be the first to hear about new
books and events.
https://heroesfootball.com/subscribe/**

Turn the page for a sneak preview of
another brilliant football story by
Matt and Tom Oldfield. . .

KANE

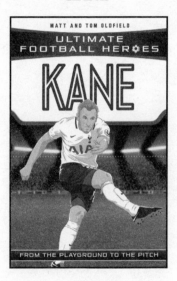

Available now!

CHAPTER 1

ENGLAND HERO

Thursday, 5 October 2017

In the Wembley tunnel, Harry closed his eyes and soaked up the amazing atmosphere. He was back at the home of football, the stadium where he had first achieved his childhood dream of playing for England. 19 March 2015, England vs Lithuania – he remembered that game like it was yesterday. He had scored that day and now, with England facing Slovenia, he needed to do it again. As England's captain and Number 9, it was his job to shoot them to the 2018 World Cup.

'Come on, lads!' Harry called out to his teammates behind him: friends like Joe Hart, Kyle Walker and

Eric Dier. It was a real honour to be their leader. With a victory over Slovenia, they would all be on their way to the biggest tournament of their lives in Russia.

Harry looked down at the young mascot by his side and smiled at him. 'Right, let's do this!'

As the two of them led the England team out onto the pitch, the fans clapped and cheered. Harry didn't look up at the thousands of faces and flags; instead, he looked down at the grass in front of him. He was totally focused on his task: scoring goals and beating Slovenia.

'If you get a chance, test the keeper,' Harry said to his partners in attack, Raheem Sterling and Marcus Rashford, before kick-off. 'I'll be there for the rebound!'

Harry's new Premiership season with Tottenham Hotspur had not begun well in August, but by September he was back to his lethal best. That month alone, he scored an incredible thirteen goals, including two goals for England against Malta. He could score every type of goal – tap-ins, headers, one-on-ones, long-range shots, penalties, even free kicks. That's what made him such a dangerous striker.

With Slovenia defending well, Harry didn't get many chances in the first half. He got in good positions but the final ball never arrived.

'There's no need to panic yet,' Harry told his teammates in the dressing room. He really didn't want a repeat of England's terrible performance against Iceland at Euro 2016. That match still haunted him. 'We're good enough to win this by playing our natural game. Be patient!'

As Ryan Bertrand dribbled down the left wing, Harry sprinted towards the six-yard box. Ryan's cross didn't reach him but the ball fell to Raheem instead. His shot was going in until a defender deflected it wide.

'Unlucky!' Harry shouted, putting his hands on his head. 'Keep going, we're going to score!'

Without this kind of strong self-belief, Harry would never have made it to the top of European football. There had been lots of setbacks along the way: rejections, disappointments and bad form. But every time, Harry bounced back with crucial goals at crucial moments. That's what made him such a superstar.

A matter of seconds later, a rebound fell to him on the edge of the penalty area. Surely, this was his moment. He pulled back his left foot and curled a powerful shot towards the bottom corner. The fans were already up on their feet, ready to celebrate. Harry never missed… but this time he did. The ball flew just wide of the post. Harry couldn't believe it. He looked up at the sky and sighed.

On the sideline, England manager Gareth Southgate cheered his team on. 'That's much better – the goal is coming, lads!'

But after ninety minutes, the goal still hadn't come. The fourth official raised his board: eight minutes of injury time.

'It's not over yet, boys!' Harry shouted, to inspire his teammates.

The Slovenian goalkeeper tried to throw the ball out to his left-back but Kyle got there first. Straight away, Harry was on the move from the back post to the front post. After playing together for years at Tottenham, they knew how to score great goals.

As Kyle crossed it in, Harry used his burst of speed to get in front of the centre-back. Again, the England supporters stood and waited anxiously. The ball was perfect and Harry stretched out his long right leg to meet it. The keeper got a touch on his shot but he couldn't keep it out.

Gooooooooooooaaaaaaaaaaaaaaaaaallllllllllllllllllllll llllll!!!!!!!!!!!!!!!!!!!!!

He had done it! Joy, relief, pride – Harry felt every emotion as he ran towards the fans. This time, he hadn't let them down. He held up the Three Lions on his shirt and screamed until his throat got sore.

'Captain to the rescue!' Kyle laughed as they hugged by the corner flag.

'No, it was all thanks to you!' Harry replied.

At the final whistle, he threw his arms up in the air. It was a phenomenal feeling to qualify for the 2018 World Cup. He couldn't wait to lead England to glory.

'We are off to Russia!' a voice shouted over the loudspeakers and the whole stadium cheered.

It was yet another moment that Harry would never forget. Against the odds, he was making his childhood dreams come true. He was the star striker for Tottenham, the club that he had supported all his life. And now, like his hero David Beckham, he was the captain of England.

Harry had never given up, even when it looked like he wouldn't make it as a professional footballer. With the support of his family and his coaches, and lots of hard work and dedication, he had proved everyone wrong to become a world-class goal machine.

It had been an incredible journey from Walthamstow to Wembley, and Harry was only just getting started.